T0114445

THE PSYCHOLOGY
OF VAMPIRES

Why have vampires become such a feature of modern culture? Can vampire-like conditions be explained by medical research? Is there a connection between vampirism and Freud?

The Psychology of Vampires presents a captivating look at the origins of vampires in myth and history and the psychological theories which try to explain why they fascinate us. It traces the development of vampires from the first-ever vampire tale, written by John Polidori in 1819, to their modern cultural legacy. Together with historical detail about Polidori's eventful life, the book also examines the characteristics of vampires and explores how and why people might identify as vampires today.

From sanguinarians who drink blood to psychic vampires who suck the energy from those around them, *The Psychology of Vampires* explores the absorbing connections between vampirism and psychology, theology, medicine and culture.

David Cohen is a psychologist, film maker, writer and a Fellow of the Royal Society of Medicine. His books include the bestselling *Diana, Death of a Goddess* on the controversies surrounding the Princess' death and *Great Psychologists as Parents*, and his film on the Soham murders was nominated for a BAFTA award.

Not suitable for younger readers

THE PSYCHOLOGY OF EVERYTHING

The Psychology of Everything is a series of books which debunk the myths and pseudo-science surrounding some of life's biggest questions.

The series explores the hidden psychological factors that drive us, from our sub-conscious desires and aversions, to the innate social instincts handed to us across the generations. Accessible, informative, and always intriguing, each book is written by an expert in the field, examining how research-based knowledge compares with popular wisdom, and illustrating the potential of psychology to enrich our understanding of humanity and modern life.

Applying a psychological lens to an array of topics and contemporary concerns – from sex to addiction to conspiracy theories – The Psychology of Everything will make you look at everything in a new way.

Titles in the series:

The Psychology of Grief
Richard Gross

The Psychology of Sex
Meg-John Barker

The Psychology of Dieting
Jane Ogden

The Psychology of Performance
Stewart T. Cotterill

The Psychology of Trust
Ken J. Rotenberg

The Psychology of Working Life
Toon W. Taris

The Psychology of Conspiracy Theories
Jan-Willem van Prooijen

For further information about this series please visit www.thepsychology ofeverything.co.uk

THE PSYCHOLOGY OF VAMPIRES

DAVID COHEN

LONDON AND NEW YORK

First published 2019
by Routledge
2 Park Square, Milton Park, Abingdon, Oxon OX14 4RN

and by Routledge
711 Third Avenue, New York, NY 10017

Routledge is an imprint of the Taylor & Francis Group, an informa business

British Library Cataloguing-in-Publication Data
A catalogue record for this book is available from the British Library

Library of Congress Cataloging-in-Publication Data
Names: Cohen, David, 1946– author.
Title: The psychology of vampires / David Cohen.
Description: 1 [edition]. | New York : Routledge, 2018. | Series: The
    psychology of everything
Identifiers: LCCN 2018015385 (print) | LCCN 2018023116 (ebook) |
    ISBN 9781351675123 (Adobe) | ISBN 9781351675116 (ePub) |
    ISBN 9781351675109 (Mobipocket) | ISBN 9781138057654
    (hardback) | ISBN 9781138057678 (pbk.) | ISBN 9781315164762
    (ebook)
Subjects: LCSH: Vampires. | Demonology. | Psychology. | Polidori,
    John William, 1795–1821.
Classification: LCC BF1556 (ebook) | LCC BF1556 .C64 2018 (print) |
    DDC 398/.45—dc23
LC record available at https://lccn.loc.gov/2018015385

ISBN: 978-1-138-05765-4 (hbk)
ISBN: 978-1-138-05767-8 (pbk)
ISBN: 978-1-315-16476-2 (ebk)

Typeset in Joanna
by Apex CoVantage, LLC

The year 2019 marks the 200th anniversary of the publication of Polidori's *The Vampyre*. It was an instant success and quickly reprinted five times. Since then the vampire has become a staple of novels, films and computer games, and also an academic subject.

CONTENTS

APERITIF – THE VAMPIRES' FAVOURITE ICE CREAM

My dearest and nearest don't understand why, when eating what Bertie Wooster called the 'eggs and b', I like a slice of blood pudding. Blood pudding was traditionally seen as a Northern working class treat. Such culinary class distinctions have been binned now. London's Goring Hotel, where Kate Middleton spent the night before she married Prince William, dishes it up as part of its full British breakfast. In the Hebrides, a Scottish variant – why not call it McBlood? – even has protected status, like cognac, champagne and camembert. France has boudin, its own version of blood pudding, laced with enough garlic to make any vampire reel.

Japan boasts a Vampire Café whose colour scheme is, of course, blood red; the basins in the toilets are stained with what looks like blood. This is very appropriate, as some myths claim the urine of vampires is red. The menus are shaped like coffins. A café in Soho in the 1960s was called the Macabre and also had coffin tables. The Japanese Vampire Cafe does not serve blood pudding, however, so it's vampire lite. My son Nicholas and I went to Romania 15 years ago and found restaurants where the waiters were dressed as vampires. A sad sign of the times; they all offered a vegetarian option.

Blood pudding is not always a savoury in these days of experimental cuisine. One company now produces black pudding ice cream, which is surely the gourmet vampire's favourite dessert.

Vampire literature has taken an academic twist recently, as it has become postmodern and third wave feminist. Buffy the Vampire Slayer is now a feminist icon and so empowered she can stuff the vampires back in their coffins and sit on the lid while flossing her total normally teeth.

One of the key distinctions today is between sanguinarians who drink blood, psychic vampires who are content merely to suck energy from those around them and hybrids who do both. The personality of vacuuming vampires who hoover energy from those they interact with has not been much studied formally. I argue that passive aggression does often involve sucking the energy of your significant others till they might as well be zombies. I offer four case histories. Vampire studies deserve credit for drawing attention to a neglected area of psychology.

Vampires lust for that most precious and symbolic of substances, blood, the liquid of life. It is so sacred that Judaism forbids the blood of animals to be consumed. Kosher slaughter drains them of it entirely before they can be cooked and eaten. So do the rules of what is halal or permitted for Muslims.

Ironically Jews have been accused of thirsting for blood like vampires. A perfect example of 'the blood libel' was the murder of an 11-year-old boy in 1141 in Norwich. Jews needed his blood to bake the Passover matzah or unleavened bread, apparently.

Nosferatu, the silent vampire film, was screened in 1922, and the Nazi propagandist Julius Streicher sat in the audience. The film gave him the idea of depicting Jews as vampires when he was in charge of Nazi propaganda. In his vile *Mein Kampf* Hitler ranted that the blood-thirsty Jews became the bloodthirsty capitalists. The Nazis were very interested in the occult.

One attraction of the vampires is their power, which has made the military use the word perhaps too freely. An RAF plane, for instance, is called the Vampire. The Honorary Chief Air Marshals since 1936 have included the future George VI, the Shah of Iran, King Hussein, the Sultan of Brunei and Prince Charles, who was promoted to the position in 2012. None of these eminences minded commanding a force which gloried in the name Vampire. A number of ships of the Royal Australian Navy are also called HMS Vampire. Since vampires can't cross water, according to some legends, this seems especially odd.

Vampires have sometimes even worn crowns. Vlad the Impaler, the fifteenth-century Romanian ruler, was a vampire who was given to every variety of murder. He was known as Dracula from around 1470. It is no accident that Dracula's first name – not his Christian name, as his actions flout every tenet of the Bible – is Vlad. Vladimir, the long version of the name, is popular again now; the latest Czar Vladimir Putin personifies the alpha male, in the eyes of his loyal followers, at least.

The great-great 16 times removed grandson of the original Impaler is the current Air Chief Marshall, the Prince of Wales. There is no evidence that Prince Charles, who allegedly used to commune with his carrots, is a vampire, but he is a fan of Transylvania and has been a regular visitor ever since 1998. He owns properties there, some of which he rents out. Sadly, I cannot report that the Prince's Trust advertises any of these as Dracula's Royal Den. Transylvania has enough lore to attract tourists without royal endorsement. There are even plans for a Dracula-world, although the investment to make it happen never quite materializes.

Vampire tourism is something of a family business. Dacre Stoker, the great-grandnephew of the author of Dracula, offers tours of sites in Romania, as does the Romanian Tourist Agency. The tours include the palace of Vlad, the original Impaler, the fortress where he started his murderous career and the town of Targoviste, where one can climb 1,460 steps up a tower bedecked with effigies of his victims.

Other must-see sites include Snagov Monastery and Huniady Castle, which holds Vlad's tomb. He died as he lived. Being beheaded in the woods around Bucharest when fighting the Turks. His enemies took his head as a war trophy, but loyal monks brought his body to the monastery to be buried. Legend says that Vlad was imprisoned in the dungeons of Huniady after being accused of treason by Matthias Corvinus, King of Hungary. The House of Dracula is in Sighisoara, the most mediaeval town in Transylvania. The cobblestone streets and colourful houses make it feel like a sixteenth-century town. UNESCO have made it a world heritage site. You can visit the yellow house where Vlad was born in 1431.

Finally, there is the lovely and also mediaeval town of Brasov, which I visited with my son Nicholas and which my mother loved. Vlad lived for some time there to keep an eye on a rival, a pretender to the throne of Wallachia. Bears sometimes wander into Brasov to scavenge the dustbins.

Vlad was a monster of cruelty. A king is rarely an outsider, but vampires are. The outsider is a personality type that has been attractive in literature for over a century. Make him a teenager, and he is even more magnetic. In the best-selling book and subsequent movie Twilight, the hero knows he is not like his classmates. It's not only his need for blood that sets him apart, but the fact he's done basic biology 40 times since he was em-vampired in 1918, when he was about to die in the influenza epidemic. Another clue that Edward Cullen is not a normal teen is that does not have acne or zits, as America calls them. Twilight's success has helped boost the vampire profile. In many public libraries there is a section devoted to Vampire DVDs. The British Library catalogue has 3,167 entries on the subject.

Some authors even describe themselves as a vampire when they have really no connection with them. In his recent Diary of a Vampire in Pyjamas, Matthias Malzieu describes his battle with a disease which makes his white blood cells melt 'like ice cubes in a bonfire'. A disease cannot be a vampire, and Malzieu does not even claim to be a psychic vampire.

The slightest hint of vampires often makes headlines. In 1990 police in Griswold, Connecticut, dug up a grave after a child had found a skull. They found more and more remains which, it soon became clear, were more than a century old. The find produced headlines. One body was astonishing. Nicholas Bellantoni, the state archaeologist, found that it had been, "had been completely . . . rearranged." The skeleton had been beheaded; the skull and thighbones rested on the ribs and vertebrae. "It looked like a skull-and-crossbones motif, a Jolly Roger. I'd never seen anything like it," Bellantoni recalled. It was the way vampires were sometimes buried.

There has been some recent violence too. In 1996 four teenagers were charged with first-degree murder after killing two parents of a cult member. The cult of some 40 western Kentucky teenagers called itself the 'Vampire Clan'. It started innocently enough. The group initially played complex games based on the role-playing game 'Vampire, the Masquerade'. They later named themselves the VAMPS for "Victorian Age Masquerade Performance Society." A new leader made the group's activities more vicious and intense. He had a history of being abused in a dysfunctional family. Under his influence the group gloried in group sex, drug use and violence. This teenager later became the youngest person on death row in the United States. The story made headlines.

Ten years later archaeologists unearthed a sixteenth-century skull in Venice; it had been buried among plague victims with a brick in its mouth. The brick was probably supposed to prevent strega – Italian vampires or witches – from leaving the grave to bite people. The story did not just make the front page of the construction trade papers. It was, again, very widely reported.

An author should explain the origin of his book. Since I saw a plaque in his honour in Soho, I have been interested in John Polidori (1795–1821), who wrote the first vampire tale and has been a little neglected since. Polidori knew the romantic poet Lord Byron, met Shelley and Mary Wollstonecraft and was an aspiring writer who was to leave an enduring cultural legacy. There have been thousands of vampire novels, but poor Poldori has so far inspired only one biography; he deserves better given all he did in his short life. While this is not a biography, I interweave aspects of his life with chapters on myth, psychology, theology (for the vampires are much like demons), medicine and culture. I try to explain why they have become such a feature of modern culture. It is not easy to find the proper tone for serious issues, fads like vampire cafes and harmless nonsense like Carry on Screaming, which stars Kenneth Williams as an electrically charged doctor. Poor Frankenstein, that it should come to this.

Chapter 1 – **Poor Poldori and the human jam** introduces the neglected author of the first vampire tale. The 'human jam', means the mingling of human remains; we all end up as marmalade for maggots. Thomas Hardy used the phrase in his poem on the old St Pancras Graveyard, whose coffins had to be moved when St Pancras station was built. Polidori's was one of the hundreds that were shifted.

Chapter 2 – **The early history of vampires** examines the prehistory of vampires, who have many fangled (and indeed fanged) cousins, nephews, nieces and blood relatives. Examples can be found going back to Babylon. The Aztecs worshipped some gods who had an insatiable thirst for blood. Martin Luther even accused the Catholic priests of being vampires in vestments, since the Eucharist involves drinking blood.

Chapter 3 – **Dracula on the couch** looks at some relevant psychology, starting with the work of Anton Mesmer. The chapter introduces Freud's ideas. As a psychiatrist, he was fascinated by the uncanny. Ernest Jones, his biographer, wrote a long paper on vampires and stressed the link with sadism. The vampire is a perfect sadist. Psychoanalysts can explain why, to their own satisfaction at least.

Chapter 4 – **The doctor who wanted to be something different** examines Polidori's early life. He wanted to be a writer but studied medicine at Edinburgh and then was employed by Byron. The most famous poet in England wanted a physician to travel with him. Byron had to flee Britain and the bailiffs and took Polidori with him. They crossed the Channel, visited the site of the Battle of Waterloo and hurtled towards Geneva to meet Shelley and Mary Wollstonecraft. Polidori, who is supposed to be the doctor, is often ill on the way. I argue there may be unsuspected reasons for the young man's illness.

Chapter 5 – **The Vampire develops, academic studies and the poet flees the bailiffs** looks at how, over time, the vampire developed from ancient Babylon to Anne Rice, the author of *Interview with a Vampire* and the *Vampire Chronicles*, who changed the way they reflected. By 2015 they are more complex than neck biters. The chapter also examines the emerging discipline of vampire studies. It is a critical survey, but I suggest that this discipline offers one important advance.

Chapter 6 – **Dip the pen in blood** gives the background to Byron's Vampire fragment, which was written on June 16, 1816, when

Byron, Shelley, Mary Wollstonecraft and Polidori were together on the shores of Lake Geneva.

Chapter 7 – **Theology, child abuse and the vampire 'syndrome'** – a proper survey has to discuss an interesting theological paradox. All demons are not vampires, but is it the case that all vampires are demons? This chapter also looks at Joan of Arc and the possible link between vampirism and child abuse.

Chapter 8 – **The first proper story** details Polidori's *The Vampyre* and the remarkable coincidence that on June 16, two staples of modern popular culture – the vampire and Frankenstein – were started.

Chapter 9 – **Sucking out energy – and the passive-aggressive personality** studies an important aspect of the personality of psychic vampires. This is also the most personal chapter, as I describe four individuals I have known who I experienced as draining my energies or, if you like, who sucked me dry.

Chapter 10 – **In print** looks at the publication of Polidori's *Vampyre* and how it became a theme and was worked and reworked in the nineteenth century, though poor Polidori only earned £30 for his work.

Chapter 11 – **Vampires on the ward** looks at medical controversies and deals with the thorny question of whether George III was one of a number of royal vampires. It has been claimed he suffered from porphyria, the disease which made him seem mad at times. Porphyria may cause a craving for blood.

Chapter 12 – **A modern Oedipus, bloodletting and three deaths** concludes the tragic life of Polidori and details how he, Shelley and Byron all died young.

Chapter 13 – **Polidori's cultural legacy** looks at the movies his work has inspired and the ways Nazis gorged on the occult and includes an analysis of the seven seasons of *Buffy the Vampire Slayer*, which have been studied in some detail as examples of 'third wave feminism'. *Abraham Lincoln: Vampire Hunter* has not been given the same treatment but shows the continuing appeal of the genre.

I hope I haven't bitten off more than I can chew.

1

POOR POLIDORI AND THE HUMAN JAM

Francis Ford Coppola directed *Bram Stoker's Dracula*. One wonders if after the horrors of *Apocalypse Now* – and Marlon Brando had some of the characteristics of a psychic vampire – Coppola wanted to have some simple fun. His Dracula careers between innocent romance and sex and gore orgies in Transylvania. My favourite postmodern blood sucker, however, is a version, *Dracula: Dead and Loving It*, dripping irony. Leslie Nielsen, the brilliant comic actor of *Police Squad* and *Naked Gun*, stars.

The author of the first vampire tale in 1816, John Polidori had little sense of irony. He desperately wanted to be a famous writer. The famous and prolific romantic poet who wrote *Don Juan*, Lord Byron had hired Polidori as his personal physician. As a result, Polidori also spent time with Madame de Stael, the publisher John Murray, the author Harriet Martineau – Queen Victoria was a fan of hers – and many others.

Polidori wrote some fair enough poems and some dreadful plays, but the only reason he is remembered now is that he wrote *The Vampyre*. A plaque in Soho at 37 Great Pulteney Street marks the house where 'poor Polidori', as many called him, lived and died. Byron's friend, John Hobhouse, mocked him as 'PollyDolly'. No called him Jolly Polly.

The Vampyre was born at the Villa Diodati on Lake Geneva. On June 16, 1816, the weather was so rough Byron, Shelley, Mary

Wollstonecraft, Polidori and Claire Claremont, one of the many women to have the hots for Byron, could not row on Lake Geneva. Cooped up inside, Byron suggested they write ghost stories. Polidori started The Vampyre and Mary Shelley Frankenstein, two key texts of modern pop and not-so-pop culture. Any relics of that night are valuable. Byron's copy of Mary Shelley's Frankenstein was valued at over £350,000 when it came up for auction in 2012. None of them would have foreseen that two centuries on, many of the themes they conjured up would be the foundation of the new field of vampirology, which is a potpourri of psychology, studies of myth and of the occult.

There is a thesis to be written on how vampire literature has boomed as belief in the afterlife has waned. Lewis Gregory, who wrote the successful gothic novel, The Monk, joined Byron and his friends in the Villa Diodati, and they debated the question of whether one could believe in vampires if one did not believe in God. Gregory doubted it, and the statistics on faith, we shall see, suggest he was right.

Polidori was 26 when he died. In 1821, at the inquest into his death, the tactful coroner attributed it to natural causes, almost certainly knowing he was lying. He wanted to spare the family pain, although the evidence showed Polidori committed suicide with prussic acid. He had been in despair for some years. Psychiatrists today would suggest he suffered from extreme depression, as the nickname 'poor Polidori' suggests. If he left a suicide note explaining his reasons, it was either not found or destroyed. He was one of many artists of the time who died young.

Even before Polidori was buried, The Vampyre became what we would now call a multimedia hit. In June 1820, Le Vampire: mélodrame en trois actes opened at the Théâtre de la Porte-Saint-Martin. Its author, James Robinson Planché, 'improved' on Polidori, with a romantic opening where the sleeping heroine, Lady Margaret, has a frightening dream about her future husband, inevitably a vampire. Two spirits, Ariel and Unda, guard Lady Margaret and chant;

> Ariel, Ariel, attend
> Listen to our magic spell

> Hither come as virtue's fiend
> And the clouds of guilt dispel.

If Lady Margaret would only heed their vision, she would never marry the toothy bloodsucker.

To spice the spooky action up even more, Planché added songs. In one, young ladies at a wedding are warned against 'angels of hell' whose "sweet voices hypnotize you." Hypnotism is a part of vampire history, as is explained in Chapter 3.

The vampire has to get a dose of blood before night falls, or he will lose his fiendish powers. It could not be said that Planché's version is subtle; the vampire's henchman is called Swill. The vampiric Lord Ruthven does not keep his haughty appearance for long. When he approaches Lady Margaret, he changes from "a young and handsome man" into a less attractive "spectre . . . frightfully distorted." He is so upset by that, he sinks into his tomb again. Vampires have their vanities.

Both Lord Ruthven and Lady Margaret also often lapse into trances. She wants to run away from her ghastly, and ghostly, future husband but cannot: "an invisible hand seemed to prevent my flight. I could not even turn mine eyes from this apparition." At the end, as her neck is bitten, Margaret shrieks 'a phantom'. She never says anything else.

The play's success set off what some critics call 'the French vampire craze' of the 1820s. Two months after Planché's play was packing them in Paris, a loose adaptation opened in London's English Opera House. Again, audiences flocked to see it.

Polidori's work even inspired an opera, Vincenzo Bellini and Felice Romani's three-act La Sonnambula. The sleepwalking heroine, Amina, is chastised for her wanderings, but it ends happily. Before she gets bitten or stabs herself like Lady Macbeth, she is declared innocent, so she can marry the noble Elvino, which makes the Swiss villagers where she lives yodel with joy.

Polidori was buried in St Pancras Old Cemetery. In the 1820s, the Old St Pancras cemetery offered grave robbers rich pickings, as medical schools needed cadavers for dissection. The Anatomy Act of

1832 finally made it possible for the schools to obtain bodies legally. The dead were not allowed to rest in peace for long, however, as they had to make way for St Pancras Station. Graves were dug up; coffins removed; headstones jammed higgledy-piggledy against an ash tree. One can still see them today.

In 1862, the assistant architect in charge of the process was the young Thomas Hardy. Even though he gave up architecture, he remained friends with the architect in charge, Arthur Blomfield. Fifteen years after they dug up the graves, they met, and Blomfield reminded him of the time they had supervised the removal of hundreds of jumbled coffins.

Their memories soon turned macabre. "Do you remember," said Blomfield, "how we found the man with two heads at St Pancras?"

Meeting Blomfield led Hardy to write a fine poem. The Levelled Churchyard is a reminder of our mortality.

"O passenger, pray list and catch
Our sighs and piteous groans,
Half stifled in this jumbled patch
Of wrenched memorial stones!"
"We late-lamented, resting here,
Are mixed to human jam,
And each to each exclaims in fear,
'I know not which I am!'"
"The wicked people have annexed
The verses on the good;
A roaring drunkard sports the text
Teetotal Tommy should!"
"Where we are huddled none can trace,
And if our names remain,
They pave some path or porch or place
Where we have never lain!"
"There's not a modest maiden elf
But dreads the final Trumpet,
Lest half of her should rise herself,

And half some local strumpet!"
"From restorations of Thy fane,
From smoothings of Thy sward,
From zealous Churchmen's pick and plane
Deliver us O Lord! Amen!"

The final version included a shocking couplet. To rhyme the 'final trumpet' (the signal of the Last Judgement) with 'sturdy strumpet' is perhaps not what either Queen Victoria or her bishops would have approved of.

Whatever his problems when he was alive, 'poor Polidori' has had a glorious posthumous career. His vampire has inspired hundreds of novels, including Bram Stoker's *Dracula*, not to mention films, comics, high art, low art and no art. His legacy also includes vampire-splattered computer games with names to curdle your spine, like *Bloodlust*, *Tales of the Raving Dead* and *The Twisted Tales of Spike McFang*.

Twilight has also been a huge hit. The heroine, Bella Swan (the name surely suggests a lovely neck) falls in love with the handsome but tortured Edward Cullen. The boy does not want to be a vampire. One of the developments of vampire fiction is that the simple villain – put him in a brain scanner and you would not find a decent neuron – Byron and Polidori created now needs therapy. That is largely due to the work of Anne Rice.

In 1973, after the death of her daughter, Rice wrote the best-selling *Interview with the Vampire*. She based her vampires on Gloria Holden's character in *Dracula's Daughter*: "It established to me what vampires were – these elegant, tragic, sensitive people. I was really just going with that feeling when writing *Interview with the Vampire*. I didn't do a lot of research." Soon after writing her novel, she developed obsessive-compulsive disorder and believed she contaminated everything she touched. She said, "What you see when you're in that state is every single flaw in our hygiene and you can't control it and you go crazy."

Rice has sold over 100 million copies of her books. Her *Interview with a Vampire* allowed vampires to look in the mirror and see themselves.

They then had to reflect on their reflection. And to reflect on the couch. And reflect on their unnatural status.

Life is like a light switch. On or off. We are dead or alive. The lure for us, but the problem for them, is that vampires are not really alive, but not really dead either. The moment Anne Rice let them see themselves in the mirror, vampires were bound to have identity issues. For us mere mortals, with vampires being undead, the idea that they are partly living raises the possibility that there is some afterlife. Freud would have called that a wish fulfilment. He argued in *The Future of an Illusion* that human beings cling to a belief in God partly because it offers hope – he never shared it – that we do not quite die. We persist with some afterlife.

Freud's illusion turned out to have some future, according to modern surveys. Though less than 10% of British adults go to church, about a third believe in 'a God'; nearly 40% believe in a higher power but not a God (20%) or don't know what they believe (14%). Younger Britons tend towards non-belief. Only 25% of 18–24-year-olds believe in a God, and 46% deny the existence of any greater spiritual power whatsoever. America is God-saturated by comparison.

Americans tend to believe in Heaven, Hell and life after death. The numbers are a little odd, but statistics often are. The question "do you believe in life after death?" gets lower positive responses than the question "do you believe in heaven?" Belief in heaven has stayed at over 8 in 10 since the late 1960s, while belief in life after death remains roughly in the range of 7 in 10. Most American Christians are sure they will live on after death, though they cannot look forward to the ecstasy of 72 virgins in Paradise, as devout Muslims can. The Church of England believes in the resurrection of the body, and so one must ask, will the vampire be resurrected as the normal human being he or she once was or in the undead state? Every culture has versions of the afterlife, though few accounts of it are as splendid as Dante's *Inferno*, the fourteenth-century epic poem where Dante is led through the circles of Hell by the Roman poet Virgil. They see the torments sinners who have indulged in lust, gluttony and heresy suffer. Polidori read the *Inferno* as a child, and it clearly made a lasting impression on him. Exploring the link between belief in God and afterlife (fading in cynical Western Europe) and interest in vampires is complex. In the USA, for example, interest remains strong both in vampires and in religion.

One of the most telling examples of the fact that faith and faith in vampires can co-exist comes from Anne Rice. In 2004, well into her vampire chronicles, she announced a trilogy of novels about Jesus. The first *Christ the Lord: Out of Egypt*, a novel about Jesus' life at age 7 won the award for the best spiritual book of the year. "This book means more to me than anything I've ever done," Rice told *Christianity Today*. "I'm not offering agnostic explanations. He is real. He worked miracles. He is the Son of God! And there is so much more to write."

The vampire offers hope. He or she is undead, not the ideal state, but much better than being stone cold dead. As long as the creature is topped up with blood and avoids vigilante Christians wandering about armed with crucifixes and a stake, the undead can go on half-living for a long time. The novelist Elisabeth Kostova believes the fascination with Dracula stems from a primitive desire to understand whether death is permanent. The Orthodox church forbids the exhumation of bodies, she discovered.

The vampire can also time travel.

It's worth reflecting on the differences between vampires and vamps. Unlike the vampire, the vamp is seductive and amusing. If you were to kiss one you would not fear for your soul. The worse that could happen is that when you got to the bedroom door, she'd smile and say, "I've got another date."

The origin of the word 'vamp', however, has nothing to do with vampires. It comes from the mediaeval French *avant-pied*, literally "before the foot," in particular the part of hose or stockings below the ankle. It became corrupted in English to *vampe*, said as two syllables, and then *vamp*.

Seductive and never quite giving up the ghost, it is no wonder the vampire has a powerful hold on both our conscious and unconscious imagination. Just like religions do.

2

THE EARLY HISTORY OF VAMPIRES

Polidori created a contradictory monster. James Twitchell argued in *The Living Dead*: "I cannot think of any other monster-molester in our culture who does such terrible things to young victims in such a gentlemanly manner. He is always polite and deferential, and his victim is almost always passive in return."

The vampire does not hack his victims to pieces. Cunningly, he persuades his prey to remove the cross that might save him or her before giving the bite, of venom not passion, which is, of course, the kiss of death. Only then can he suck the blood which makes him tingle with life. Sucked dry, the victim now faces a fate worse than death and turns into a vampire, condemned to find new necks.

Neck, suck, bite – talk of vampires is charged with suppressed sexuality. The vampire is indeed a vamp.

Stoker's Dracula even had spiritual pretensions. He paraphrased Christ's words. "He that eateth my flesh and drinketh my blood, dwelleth in me, and I in him." In the 1931 film where Bela Lugosi gave a superbly hammy performance, Dracula rips open a vein above his heart and forces Mina to drink his blood. As she drinks, Dracula exclaims in best Biblical style, "Now you shall be flesh of my flesh, and blood of my blood." Mina is prepared to do this, as Dracula is far more attractive than her fiancé Jonathan Harker, who hopes to become a solicitor.

In 1936, Universal released a sequel. Despite his apparent death in the 1931 film, Orlok (presumably fortified by vintage blood) returned to life in three more films: the 1936 sequel, a 1945 film and a parody by Abbott and Costello.

The vampire had a long prehistory by the time Polidori wrote him. In the Babylonian epic *Gilgamesh*, the Ekimmu, or Departed Spirit, was the soul of a dead person who could find no rest and was always looking for fresh new blood. The Ekimmu was rather naïve, imagining a good bite would bring him everlasting peace. To surprise his prey, the Ekimmu had the useful ability of being able to waft through windows, doors and walls, materialize and pounce.

There are many demons, but no vampires, in the Bible. In Jewish lore, Lilith was a demon who drank the blood of babies. In *To Love a Vampire* by Sarita Irwin, a routine vampire novel, Lilith seduces an innocent boy in Biblical Canaan. After lashings of intense sex, she turns him into a vampire. He remains undead for centuries and then becomes an American. He seduces Sandra, a New York woman who could have been a character in *Sex in the City*. Soon after she meets the immortal Arthur, they are frothing in bed. It is worth quoting part of a key scene;

> Oh Christ, Sandra gasped raising and lowering her hips faster and faster. I'm being used like a lump of meat. This is the lowest degradation I have ever felt.

And Sandra had had a few disastrous experiences.

> "You're different from other women I've known," Arthur grunted pounding into her.

Let us have a moment of reader involvement. As a test, try grunting that sentence. It's not so easy. I found myself spitting and spitting while pounding is not very sexy. Having grunted, and "proceeded to peak, unleashing the seminal contents of his body into her," Arthur agrees to stay with her all night, during which Sandra becomes a vampire.

Ancient Greek mythology had a number of blood-drinking monsters, but none were undead. In Homer's *Odyssey*, they had other problems; they were too insubstantial to be heard by the living. To beef up their voices a few decibels, they needed a glug of blood.

The Aztecs' many gods needed far more than a pint a day. The Aztecs would go to war just to find people to sacrifice. It couldn't be any old ragtag and bobtail human specimen. The disabled weren't good enough and were sent to work the silver mines. Some complained of discrimination. Cruel as Aztec culture seems to have been, it was not physiologically daft. To keep the gods happy, human beings had to give them the liquid of life. Many goddesses were similar to vampires. Tlalteuctli, was usually portrayed as an enormous toad with blood-covered jaws. Not the most divine appearance.

Across the Pacific, the people of Bali were more interested in teeth, as they were the first to use tooth sharpening, or tooth filing. They also stained some of their teeth. The Wapare tribe in Africa had the idea of frightening enemies by making their teeth resemble dangerous predators like sharks.

Blood and bones, the basics of life, give rise to strange customs, nowhere more than in Eastern Europe, birthplace to Freud and vampires. My mother, who was born in Romania, told me that it was traditional to exhume the dead seven years after they had been buried, oil their bones to get rid of the maggots, and inter them again. (Luckily she did not expect me to do this!) Romania is, of course, Dracula-central. So is neighbouring Hungary, one of whose aristocrats had a part to play in the story.

Elizabeth Bathory was a sixteenth-century Hungarian countess who was the first person to be found guilty of 'vampirism'. Her family was one of the noblest in Transylvania. She married another aristocrat, but he did not satisfy her, and she took a peasant lover. When her husband found out, he had the man castrated and then torn to pieces by dogs. She was 43 when her violent husband died – and now she was free to please herself, which she did in cascades of blood.

Elizabeth could not keep her sadistic activities secret forever, though. Word got out that she enjoyed torturing and killing young girls. Nobody was too bothered as long as her victims were just her servants, but then she started to kill girls sent to her by local families to learn good manners. If someone founded The Vampire Academy of Devilish Decorum, it would attract many students today. Drinking the blood of young girls was better than Botox; it would preserve her youthfulness and her looks, Elizabeth believed. She was accused of stabbing her victims, biting their breasts, cutting their flesh with scissors, sticking needles into their lips and burning them with red-hot irons.

Eventually, a Lutheran minister became suspicious and, in 1610, he demanded an investigation. Elizabeth was arrested, and so were four of her favourite servants. Three were executed. Elizabeth herself was too grand to be put on trial, but she was shut up in Csetje Castle in solitary confinement. All the blood did not make her live that long; she died at the age of 54.

In seventeenth-century Britain, the fearful entities were ghosts and witches, not vampires. The ghost of Hamlet's father echoes the Bible with his line "Remember me"; in *Macbeth*, the three witches watch their cauldron hubble bubble. Vampires, however, never set foot on Shakespeare's stage. He had written his last play when William Harvey discovered that the heart was, in fact, a blood pump. Oddly that did not spark any English interest in vampires.

Germany was different. Seventeenth-century stories of the *Nachzehrer*, or 'after-devourers', also suggest they were anatomically aware at this period. The after-devourers chewed on their burial shrouds. As the body decomposes, bacterial growth in the soft tissues bloats it. So-called decomposition fluids from the lungs leak, and this is called 'Purge fluid'. It could make the shroud sag or even burst, creating the illusion that a still partly living corpse had been chewing it. In a 1679 tract, a Protestant theologian accused the after-devourers of coming out of their coffins and attacking their surviving family members. Vampires understandably resent the living. People could stop that by exhuming the body and stuffing its mouth with soil, a stone and a coin. Unable to chew, the corpse would die all over again of starvation.

Until 1734, 'vampyre' did not exist even as a word in English, according to the Oxford English Dictionary, which states it first appeared in the book Travels of Three English Gentlemen. Another account says it was first used in a periodical called The Craftsman. The word became popular because a grisly drama gripped Europe.

In 1731, 13 people died in a Serbian village. The authorities in Vienna were not going to rely on the evidence of credulous peasants, so they sent Dr Glaser, a specialist in infectious diseases, to investigate. Glaser, being rational, blamed the deaths on malnutrition, but the villagers insisted vampires had bitten the 13 to death. The vampires had to be 'executed', or they would kill again. Glaser exhumed the corpses. To his surprise, he found most were not decomposed; many were swollen and still had blood in their mouths. He had the bodies reburied.

Vienna imagined Glaser had lost his mind and demanded a second opinion. They sent a military surgeon, Johann Flückinger, two colonels and, to be sure no one got bamboozled, two other doctors. On January 7, the squad of experts opened the graves again. They were staggered. Twelve corpses were still not decayed. There was fresh blood, and the viscera were 'in good condition'. Some corpses even looked plump. The doctors stated the bodies were in 'the vampiric condition'. To make sure the undead finally died, they cut off the heads of the 'vampires'.

Two weeks later, Glaser's father, a Viennese doctor, who wrote for the Nuremberg journal Commercium Litterarium, sent its editors a letter describing the case. The story aroused huge interest.

Three years later, more mystery: a soldier called Arnold Paole claimed he had been plagued by a vampire near modern day Kosovo. He had apparently saved himself by eating soil from the vampire's grave and smearing himself with blood. Paole didn't survive long, though, as he fell from a wagon, broke his neck and died. Soon after, four people complained they had been plagued by Paole, who had now become a vampire himself. The four themselves did not last long.

When the villagers opened Paole's grave, they found his corpse was undecomposed "and fresh blood had flowed from his eyes, nose, mouth and ears. The old nails on his hands and feet, along with the skin, had fallen off, and new ones had grown." Paole groaned and bled. The villagers drove a stake through his heart and then burned his body. Ashes can't bite your neck, they reckoned.

These cases inspired 34 learned publications over the next three years. Getting the geography a bit wrong, the London press reported that in Hungary there were "dead bodies sucking the blood of the living, for the latter visibly dry up, while the former are filled with blood." By the middle of the eighteenth century vampires were fashionable – the Earl of Sandwich even named a racehorse Vampire.

One very learned publication which Polidori, Byron and the rest of the group at the Villa Diodati read was Dom Augustin Calmet's (1746) *Dissertations upon the Apparitions of Angels, Daemons and Ghosts, and Concerning the Vampires of Hungary, Bohemia, Moravia and Silesia.*

The church was worried by this vampire mania. By the mid-eighteenth century, Pope Benedict XIV sensibly declared that vampires were a fallacy. The Hapsburg Empress Maria Theresa also put vampire beliefs down as 'superstition and fraud'. Pope and Empress might as well . . . well since Thomas Hardy used it, I will follow his example . . . they might as well have been pissing in the wind.

Vampires finally crossed the Atlantic in June 1784, when Moses Holmes of Wilmington wrote to the editor of the *Connecticut Courant and Weekly Intelligencer.* He warned of "a certain Quack Doctor, a foreigner" (not Johnny Foreigner, it seems, but Johannes Foreigner), who urged families to dig up and burn dead relatives to stop 'consumption', the name then given to tuberculosis. Several children were exhumed at this doctor's request, and Holmes wanted no more of it. He wrote: "And that the bodies of the dead may rest quiet in their graves without such interruption, I think the public ought to be aware of being led away by such an imposture."

The French Revolution of 1789 and, especially, the horrors of the guillotine, boosted interest in terror. Jane Austen in *Northanger Abbey* satirized the gothic novel, and its success;

> Dear creature! how much I am obliged to you; and when you have finished *Udolpho*, we will read *The Italian* together; and I have made out a list of ten or twelve more of the same kind for you.

Have you, indeed! How glad I am! — What are they all?

I will read you their names directly; here they are, in my pocket-book. *Castle of Wolfenbach, Clermont, Mysterious Warnings, Necromancer of the Black Forest, Midnight Bell Orphan of the Rhine,* and *Horrid Mysteries.* Those will last us some time.

Yes, pretty well; but are they all horrid, are you sure they are all horrid?

Yes, quite sure; for a particular friend of mine, a Miss Andrews, a sweet girl, one of the sweetest creatures in the world, has read every one of them.

Northanger Abbey was only published — by Byron's publisher, John Murray — in 1817, the year after Jane Austen died. Since writers are allowed their fancies, I wonder what she would have written if Murray had escorted her to the Villa Diodati. Would we have *Sense and Superstition? Pride and the Poltergeist?*

Eighteenth-century America became fretful about vampires. Michael Bell, a Rhode Island folklorist and author of *Food for the Dead,* has studied about 80 exhumations, reaching as far back as the late 1700s. Most took place in New England. Vampire panics, Bell argues, are not inexplicable. They almost always occurred in the midst of tuberculosis epidemics. By the 1800s, when these scares were at their height, 'consumption' was responsible for almost a quarter of all deaths in New England. The vampire tales were an attempt to cope. "People find themselves in dire situations, where there's no recourse through regular channels," Bell said. "The folk system offers an alternative, a choice."

Some towns in Maine and Massachusetts flipped the exhumed 'vampire' face down in the grave so the body could do no more mischief. In Connecticut, Rhode Island and Vermont, they often burned the heart, sometimes inhaling the smoke as a cure for tuberculosis. In 1830, in Manchester, hundreds flocked to a heart-burning ceremony at a blacksmith's forge: "Timothy Mead officiated at the altar in the sacrifice to the Demon Vampire who it was believed was still sucking the blood of the then living wife of Captain Burton," according to the town's history.

Brian Carroll, a history professor at Central Washington University, believes such anti-vampire rituals were introduced during the American Revolution by German doctors. The New England vampires assumed some of the characteristics of the German *Nachzehrer*, so they stayed in their graves, harming the living through 'sympathetic magic'. Bell, however, believes that the New England vampires were more like their Romanian cousins as they "were looking for liquid blood in the vital organs, not evidence of shroud chewing." The remedies of "cutting the heart out, burning it to ashes, and giving the ashes to the sick person or sick people" had been practiced in Romania.

From the mid-eighteenth century, vampire lore and fiction made a significant contribution to political debate. Critics compared governments to bloodsuckers. Tax was a way to gratify the 'fat gutted vampire' that the authorities were. Then, Friedrich Engels referred to 'the vampire property-holding class' in *The Condition of the Working Class in England*. His friend, Karl Marx, saw the propaganda possibilities. He now used vampires to represent the bourgeoisie's greed. He adopted the image almost obsessively. (Ironically, Engels was a property owner himself, and the profits of his factory subsidized Marx for years.) Marx used the vampire insult in his analysis of class warfare. The bourgeoisie was an ever-restless class because it suffered a thirst that could never be quenched. Marx did not say it was blood, of course, but he contrasted 'living labour' with the dead or 'accumulated' labour embodied in machinery and raw materials – in short, in capital itself. These days the imagery is more bird-like; we talk of bankers being vultures rather than vampires and of being bled dry by rapacious interest and charges for every fiddly financial operation one can imagine.

In 1845, vampire literature took a turn for the worse. *Varney the Vampire* sounds like the title of a bad comic – and in many ways it was. It has sometimes been described as the worst book of the nineteenth century. Its 600,000 words dull the reader with maddening repetitions. If you say something, James Rymer, the author, seems to have believed – why not say it five times? None of that stopped it being a success, and as one critic sniped, "the most influential vampire story that nobody reads."

Varney is not handsome or seductive; he looks sallow and sports protruding fangs and extended fingernails. He also lacks the vampire edge, as he is slow, so his victims often have time to scream for help as they wake to find him biting their necks. Often Varney has to leg it, as angry friends and relatives storm into the bedroom and discover him at work.

Varney is also vulnerable and can be hit or shot by rescuers, who aren't waving crucifixes or pelting him with garlic. He can, however, regenerate by moonlight. Rymer seems to have muddled up vampires and werewolves. Varney does not do well in water, though. Rivers and oceans invariably spew back his body. He is too damned for water, often a symbol of forgiveness, to heal him.

Until 1873, vampires, apart from Elizabeth Bathory, were male. That year, Le Fanu produced the first female vampire, Carmilla, which he presented as part of the casebook of Dr Hesselius. The heroine, Laura, grows up in a 'picturesque and solitary' castle with her father, a wealthy English widower. When she is 6, Laura has a vision of a beautiful visitor in her bedroom.

Twelve years later, Laura's father tells her of a letter from his friend, General Spielsdorf.

The General was supposed to bring his niece, Bertha Rheinfeldt, to visit. But Bertha died in suspicious circumstances. Instead a carriage accident brings the mysterious Carmilla and her mother to the castle door. Carmilla and Laura are the same age; each girl recognizes the other because Carmilla also dreamed a beautiful girl when she was 6.

Carmilla's mother leaves her daughter at the castle with warnings that echo Ruthven's. Don't say a word about yourself or the family, or the doom will be upon you. The girls become close friends. Carmilla is enigmatic; her moods change for no apparent reason. Le Fanu then adds a diabolical flourish, as Carmilla never joins the household in its prayers, and she also sleepwalks. She even tries to seduce Laura. This is the first overtly gay moment in vampire fiction.

Laura's sleep is also disturbed. She has nightmares of a large cat-like beast biting her on the chest. The beast then changes into a woman and disappears through the door without opening it. In another nightmare, Laura hears a voice say, "Your mother warns you to beware of the assassin." Suddenly Carmilla is at the foot of her bed, her nightdress drenched in blood.

After all this spookiness, Laura finds a portrait of her ancestor, Mircalla, Countess Karnstein, dated 1698. The Countess looks just like Carmilla. Her father takes Laura to the village of Karnstein. On the way they meet General Spielsdorf, who reveals his own traumatic story. At a ball, some years previously, Spielsdorf and his niece Bertha had met a young woman named Millarca and her enigmatic mother. The mother asked the General to let Millarca stay with them for three weeks while she went to deal with a secret matter of great importance.

Bertha then falls ill, suffering the same symptoms as Laura. After consulting a doctor, the General realized a vampire was attacking Bertha. Arming himself with a sword, he hid and waited. Then a large black creature crawled into his Bertha's bed and started on her neck. When the General attacked the beast, he saw it looked like Millarca. She fled through the locked door, unharmed. Bertha died immediately afterwards.

As Carmilla is a vampire, she is not easy to get rid of. She turns up in a church and rages at the General, who has come armed with an axe. Carmilla is inevitably strong as an ox, disarms the General and disappears. The General then explains to his daughter that Carmilla is also Millarca, both anagrams for the original name of the vampire Mircalla.

Baron Vordenburg, one of whose ancestors rid the area of vampires long ago, then appears. In a twist that suggests Le Fanu knew of the vampire dramas of the 1730s, an Imperial Commission exhumes the vampire's body. It is breathing faintly, its heart is beating, its eyes are open, blood is everywhere. A stake is driven through the heart of the undead Millarca/Carmilla, and her head is struck off. Both are burned, and the ashes are thrown into a river. Unlike Varney, Le Fanu's story is readable.

A real case now made vampires even more popular, that of Lena Mercy Brown. She lived – and died – in Exeter, Rhode Island. By 1892, the year she died, Exeter's population had fallen to just 961, from more than 2,500 in 1820. Tuberculosis was ravaging the remaining families.

Lena's family began to die from the disease in December 1882. Lena's mother was the first to perish. Lena's sister, Mary Olive, a 20-year-old dressmaker, died the next year. A few years later, Lena's brother Edwin fell ill and had the good sense to leave for Colorado Springs, hoping that the climate would improve his health.

Lena was just a child when her mother and sister died, and she did not fall ill until nine years after they were buried. A doctor attended her in "her last illness" and told her father "that further medical aid was useless." the *Providence Journal* wrote. All they could do was pray. Some neighbours wanted more than prayers. Several approached Lena's father and suggested the deaths were supernatural. Perhaps an unseen diabolical force was preying on his family, a force that was also capricious. It could be that one of the three Brown women wasn't actually dead and instead was secretly feasting "on the living tissue and blood of Edwin," the *Providence Journal* wrote. Neighbours asked to exhume the bodies so they could kill the vampires for good. George Brown agreed.

On March 17, 1892, the bodies were dug up as the family doctor and a *Providence Journal* correspondent looked on. Ten years dead, Lena's sister and mother were barely more than bones. Lena's body, though, "was in a fairly well-preserved state. The heart and liver were removed, and in cutting open the heart, clotted and decomposed blood was found." The doctor stressed that Lena's lungs showed 'diffuse tuberculous germs'. The villagers were in no mood for scientific explanations; they burned her heart and liver on a nearby rock.

These days millions of us watch pathology porn without needing to know the intricacies of what happens to our bodies. Seven days after death, most of the body is discoloured, and giant blood-tinged blisters begin to appear. As the internal organs and the fatty tissues decay, they produce large quantities of foul-smelling gas. By the second week a bloody fluid seeps out of the mouth and nose. After three to four weeks, the grossly swollen internal organs begin to rupture and eventually liquefy and can produce the 'decomposed blood' found in Lena Brown's coffin.

The exhumation, typically, made news all over the world. A well-known anthropologist, George Stetson, went to Rhode Island to probe 'the barbaric superstition'. When he published his findings in the *American Anthropologist*, strange theories bubbled in their wake. Oscar Wilde had just published *The Picture of Dorian Gray*; maybe such 'neurotic' modern novels were fuelling the New England madness. Incest also seemed possible, a writer said in the *Boston Daily Globe*, as "perhaps the frequent intermarriage of families in these back country districts may partially account for some of their characteristics." Incest would feature in many vampire tales.

The Victorians were a good audience for virtually any occult material. Any ectoplasm would do, one might say. The Society for Psychical Research was set up in 1882 to investigate mesmeric, psychical and 'spiritualist' phenomena "in a purely scientific spirit." Its first president was Henry Sidgwick, professor of moral philosophy at Cambridge. His collaborators included the physicist Lord Rayleigh and Arthur Balfour, who was prime minister from 1902–1905.

From the 1850s onwards, séances were popular; celebrity mediums came from America to England; photography seemed to offer proof of survival after death, with pictures of ectoplasm, some relic of the dead streaming from the bodies of the living. The camera did not lie, the public believed, not realizing how it could be manipulated.

Many great Victorian novels worked the supernatural. Ghosts feature in *A Christmas Carol* by Charles Dickens, in *Wuthering Heights* by Emily Bronte and in *An Account of Some Strange Disturbances in Augier Street* by Sheridan Le Fanu. Perhaps the most brilliant is Henry James's *The Turn of the Screw* (1890), whose brother William wrote *The Varieties of Religious Experience* and was a member of the American Society for Psychical Research. The central characters are a governess (Miss Jessel), two slightly creepy children (Miles and Flora) and their dealings with chilling ghosts, specifically one named Peter Quint, who appears to one of the girls and makes her turn cold. Benjamin Britten turned The Turn of the Screw into an opera, testifying to its enduring appeal.

Conan Doyle, the creator of Sherlock Holmes, became one of the most devoted members of the Society for Psychical Research. He wrote The Case for Spirit Photography.

In 1917, two teenage girls in Yorkshire produced two photographs of fairies. The setting was pure fantasy, a country garden with a waterfall where four fairies dance; three have wings, the fourth plays a long flute-like instrument. Conan Doyle accepted the photos as genuine evidence for fairies and wrote The Coming of the Fairies (1922).

Science was offering discoveries such as magnetic fields, radiation, radio waves, electrical currents and the first motor car, so paranormal researchers suggested that the occult operated in similar ways. Marie Curie, who did some of the first research into uranium, attended séances to assess the powers of mediums. The British physicist J. J. Thomson, who demonstrated the existence of the electron in 1897, and Lord Rayleigh, who won the 1904 Nobel Prize in Physics, also attended séances. This was ironic, given that 40 years after Darwin had published On the Origin of the Species, many intellectuals were uncertain the truths of religion. Bram Stoker, author of the famous Dracula, dramatized aspects of this tension between faith and science but in a complicated way, as we shall see.

At Trinity College in Dublin, Stoker had been taught English literature by Edward Dowden, the biographer of Shelley. As a result, he had studied the events at the Villa Diodati in detail and lectured on the subject.

To make a living, while he was a student, Stoker wrote theatre reviews. He met Dion Boucicault, the French playwright who had written his first play when he was 18. It opened in in 1838. In the 1850s, he wrote A Legend of the Devil's Dyke, the story of Megan, who is pursued by a deserter from the army who has many vampire traits. Megan is luckier than most, as the man she loves kills the deserter before he can kill her.

By 1872 Stoker had learned from Dowden about the origins of the vampire and knew of two plays based on Polidori's work – Planché's adaptation in 1820 and Boucicault's Legend of the Devil's Dyke. Yet vampires were not his priority, however, as it would take him over 25 years to actually write Dracula. The reason they were not his priority was that in 1876 he met the famous actor Henry Irving, who invited him to come to London to be the business manager of the Lyceum theatre. Stoker would work for Irving until the actor's death.

Some theatre historians believe Stoker both loved and hated Irving. Nina Auerbach (1998) has pointed out in his biography of the great actress Ellen Terry: "Always there was something perverse about Irving, not only crafty but cruel." In his Reminiscences, Stoker talked about "the magnetism of his genius." Irving never played Dracula, but Stoker saw him play Mephistopheles in Marlowe's Dr Faustus 762 times, more than he played any other part. Dracula has much of Mephistopheles in him.

The other event which needs to be noted are the murders committed by Jack the Ripper in Whitechapel at the end of the 1880s. Some Ripperologists, as they call themselves, have argued he was a vampire. Blood was certainly in the air when Stoker published Dracula in 1896, the book which gave Polidori's vampire a fresh lease of life.

Dracula highlights the contrast between the 'superstitious' East (Transylvania, where Johnny Foreigner lurks dastardly) and the 'modern' sweet-as-roses West, which welcomes scientific progress. In London, Mina practices on the typewriter so she can help her dull fiancé, Jonathan Harker, when he returns from Dracula-land. The young doctor Dr John Seward records his diary on a phonograph. Dracula threatens that modernity.

Leaving Harker at his mediaeval castle, Dracula comes to London. He bites and bleeds "please don't let me be a virgin for another night" Lucy Westenra. Her three would-be lovers summon the world's leading expert on diseases of the blood, Dr Abraham Van Helsing. He and Seward try to help Lucy by giving her transfusions, which was then a new and risky procedure. Modern medicine is no match for Dracula's powers, however. So Van Helsing resorts to the 'superstitious' and places garlic around Lucy's bed. He is too late, though, and she becomes a vampire. In the movies she has what could be called a 'wow' orgasm, writhing like a snake in ecstasy. To a modern reader, Lucy is in fact a frustrated teen who is desperate for any excuse to have sex, which as a nice rich girl, she should not be interested in.

Stoker then brings faith to the rescue. Only Christian symbols seem to stop Dracula and Lucy from killing more people. When Van Helsing places the Host wafer on Mina's head to bless her, "[t]here was a fearful scream which almost froze our hearts to hear. As he had placed the Wafer on Mina's forehead, it had seared it – had burned into the flesh as though it had been a piece of white-hot metal." The Christian symbol is too strong for the 'unclean' Mina, who is slowly changing into a vampire herself. The crucifix had become the fix.

Stoker added elements that had never previously featured in tales of vampires – the weakness to garlic and wolfbane, the hatred of the cross and other holy items, the need to sleep in their native soil, the inability to cross moving water. He also invented the nice touch that vampires love silver – Marx would have approved – and the fact that vampires are not reflected in mirrors. One must have a soul to see oneself. When he is shaving and looking in the mirror, Harker feels a hand on his shoulder, and hears Dracula saying "Good-morning." "But there was no reflection of him in the mirror!" Harker cuts himself, and the blood excites Dracula.

Carefully, Stoker makes clear that Dracula lusts for Harker. It was understandable that he was wary, as he began writing *Dracula* only a month after Oscar Wilde was convicted of sodomy and sent to Reading Jail. Talia Schaffer, in a "'A Wilde Desire Took Me': The Homoerotic History of *Dracula*," says, "Wilde's influence on Stoker has been neglected partly because much of Stoker's biographical information has disappeared" – like many letters of Byron, as we shall see.

Though Stoker added many new touches, his Dracula had many similarities to earlier vampires. He exhibits superhuman strength. Harker describes how Dracula "caught my arm in a grip of steel; his strength must have been prodigious." Dracula is also prone to lapse into trance states. His gaze paralyses or hypnotizes would-be victims with a "blaze of basilisk horror." Stoker's brother, the surgeon sir William Thornley Stoker, reviewed and annotated early drafts of *Dracula* to make them medically accurate.

Professor Nicholas Groom of Exeter University suggests that passages in *Dracula* mirror contemporary medical descriptions of how 'real life' vampires behaved. Dracula's female vampire, for example, makes the same 'churning' sound with her tongue as is described in academic medical treatises.

The phenomenal success of *Dracula* prompted Ernst Jensch's 1906 essay, *On the Psychology of the Uncanny*. It is time to examine how psychologists responded to the many fictions in which the vampire was both villain and, sometimes, hero.

3

DRACULA ON THE COUCH

Is it pure chance that in 1896, when Stoker wrote *Dracula*, Freud started the self-analysis which led him to develop psychoanalysis? Definitely maybe is the best conclusion. One must remember that Freud shared one skill with vampires; he was a good hypnotist. Hypnotism was an important feature of the way psychology and psychiatry developed in the late eighteenth and nineteenth century. Though Anton Mesmer never used the word hypnotism, his work provoked much interest in what we now recognize as hypnotism.

Mesmer studied medicine at the University of Vienna in 1759. In 1766, his *On the Influence of the Planets on the Human Body* examined the influence of the moon and the planets on the human body, and, building on Newton's theory of the tides, he considered the possibility that the sun and the moon might produce tides in the body too. This work led him to claim that an invisible force, 'animal magnetism', existed. Controlling it would make it possible to cure hysteria and other mental problems.

Mesmer made his first patient, the hysterical Francisca Österlin, swallow a preparation containing iron and then attached magnets to her body. She felt streams of a mysterious fluid running through her body, she said. And her symptoms disappeared for several hours at least.

Mesmer established intense contact. He would sit in front of his patient, press the patient's thumbs in his hands and stare into the patient's eyes. He ran his hands down their arms. He pressed his fingers on an area below the diaphragm, sometimes holding his hands there for hours. To add yet more drama, Mesmer would often conclude his treatments by playing some soothing music. The French King Louis XVI appointed a very high-powered commission to investigate. One of its members was Benjamin Franklin, the American ambassador to France, who did pioneering work on electricity, not to mention being one of the Founding Fathers; another was the so-called father of chemistry, Antoine Lavoisier, who recognized and named oxygen in 1778 and hydrogen in 1783. The commission was critical. Lavoisier claimed Mesmer's results had more to do with suggestion than with any invisible magical force. Then the Marquis de Puységur, whose estates produced some the best Armagnac in France, discovered that he could get identical results by inducing a peaceful, sleep-like trance. There was no need for magnets or convulsions.

Patients would obey Puységur and even speak while in a trance. They could follow instructions given during the trance – and say their symptoms had gone – even after Puységur snapped them out of it. He was amazed, however, to find his subjects could not remember what had happened while in the trance. He had discovered the power of suggestibility and of hypnotism. Vampires would turn out to be master hypnotists, sometimes, as they were able to put their victims in trances and bend them to their usually evil will.

The most astonishing demonstration of the power of hypnosis came in the mid-nineteenth century. James Esdaile was a surgeon in India. He needed something that is now routine but did not exist then, an effective anaesthetic. Having read Mesmer, he wondered if his technique might help. On April 4, 1845, he performed his first mesmeric procedure on a patient who had found a previous operation on his scrotum unbearably painful. Esdaile wrote;

> I have a great mind to try it on this man, but as I never saw it prac-
> tised, and know it only from reading, I shall probably not succeed.

Esdaile was not a quick hypnotist; his 'mesmeric act' was an exhausting procedure, according to the Scottish doctor and philosopher James Braid. It was Braid who seems to have first used the word 'hypnotism'.

> Esdaile's method was to make the patient lie down in dark room, wearing only a loin cloth, and [Esdaile would] repeatedly pass the hands in the shape of claws, slowly over the [patient's] body, within one inch of the surface, from the back of the head to the pit of the stomach, breathing gently on the head and eyes all the time [and] he seems to have sat behind the patient, leaning over him almost head to head and to have laid his right hand for extended periods on the pit of the stomach.

Esdaile became famous for painless surgery, especially in cases of the scrotal 'tumours' that were in common in Bengal at that time; the disease was transmitted by mosquitoes. Esdaile's mesmeric anaesthesia turned to be extremely safe as he claimed in his 1846 *Mesmerism in India, and its Practical Application in Surgery and Medicine*.

The Viceroy, who ruled India in Queen Victoria's name, set up a committee to investigate. He appointed the Inspector General of Hospitals as its chairman and nine others, including the Surgeon to the Native Hospital. Their tasks were to see if Esdaile's results were real and if the primitive natives were more susceptible to hypnosis. The committee studied 10 of his surgical cases and concluded he had not faked the results. His discovery became irrelevant, though, when ether started to be used as an anaesthetic a decade later, as it was far simpler than hypnosis.

Esdaile's work, however, remained a landmark and was known to Jean Marie Charcot, the most famous neurologist of the era, who was also interested in hypnosis. Freud studied with Charcot at the Salpetriere in Paris in 1885 and was so awed he had to take cocaine to fortify himself every time he was invited to a soiree at Charcot's house. Freud used hypnotism in his early work and also knew of Esdaile's achievements.

A much less famous doctor was a more obscure link between Polidori and psychoanalysis. William Carpenter had also qualified at Edinburgh, studied thinking and also saw that unconscious prejudices could be stronger than conscious thought and that they were more dangerous as a result. Carpenter worked with William Hamilton, who argued that the mind contains far more 'mental furniture' than consciousness reveals. Hamilton wrote, "the sphere of our conscious modifications is only a small circle in the centre of a far wider sphere of action and passion of which we are only conscious through its effects."

Carpenter gathered evidence for what he called 'unconscious cerebration'. He cited cases where people recalled knowledge they did not know they possessed. Emotional reactions can occur, Carpenter said, outside of consciousness until attention is drawn to them:

> Our feelings towards persons and objects may undergo most important changes, without our being in the least degree aware, until we have our attention directed to our own mental state, of the alteration which has taken place in them.

Carpenter clearly anticipated Freud's thinking. It was only a small step from the unconscious to the uncanny. In his 1906 paper, Ernst Jentsch saw the uncanny as a product of 'intellectual uncertainty' – and vampires illustrated that. What is more uncertain that the question of whether one is living, dead or undead?

Freud took Jentsch's title for a paper of his own. He devoted a large part of it to the origins of the German word 'unheimlich', which is more accurately translated as 'unhomely' than uncanny. This, Freud argued, feeds on unresolved childhood anxieties and unconsciously reminds us of our forbidden, repressed impulses and fears – including the terror of death. His followers embellished and suggested vampires wanted revenge for some trauma, which explains why they have to bite – the most primitive form of aggression.

Freud's ideas on the uncanny must be put in some context. Every child goes through a series of fixed psychosexual stages which Freud labelled the oral, anal, phallic, latency and genital. The name of each stage, apart from latency, highlights the area of the body which is then the main source of pleasure but also the main potential source of frustration. At the oral stage the baby is all mouth. He or she gets satisfaction from putting objects into it. Babies suck, breastfeed and bite. In doing so they pander to the infantile 'id', which for Freud represented the wildest primitive instincts. The pleasures of the baby id are oral, and this could lead to an oral fixation.

Infants who are not well fed may become orally fixated. Typically, Freud also suggested that if a baby is too well fed, that could also lead to oral fixation. The orally frustrated baby might become a psychologically dependent adult who was always trying to make up for what he or she was denied in infancy. They develop into highly manipulative persons too.

Freud himself smoked cigars even after he developed cancer of the jaw. He needed oral stimulation and often said he could not think if he did not smoke. A doctor who smoked was more acceptable than one who bit his nails or sucked his thumbs while listening to his patients.

As a young doctor, Freud had to do military service and worked in the army. He retained a fondness for military metaphors and compared the mind to an army on the march. The troops represented the libido, which is not just the sex drive, as often assumed, but something like a life force. As they advance, the enemy attacks. If the Freudian forces, as one might describe them, win the battle and resolve the conflict of the psychosexual stage they are in, most troops can move on to the next battle, which is, in fact, the next stage of psychosexual development. If they do not succeed, more troops have to remain behind to fight. So only fewer troops, or a weaker libido, can march on to the next stage. A healthy libido will advance to the phallic stage and also desire the right object to love, someone of the opposite sex. Freud did not condemn homosexuality but said it was no great boon either when a mother asked him to cure her son of what she saw as a perversion.

The libido could get in a tangle and, even to steal Hardy's phrase, in a 'human jam'. One of Freud's favourite patients was Princess Marie

Bonaparte, Napoleon's great grandniece, who helped bring up Prince Charles' father, the Duke of Edinburgh. The princess consulted Freud because none of her lovers satisfied her. At least two were French prime ministers. Her husband, the brother of the King of the Hellenes, had a particularly tangled libido, as he was in love with his uncle. Freud persuaded Marie not to sleep with her son, which she thought might finally satisfy her. When the troops were bogged down, the development of the libido was stalled. The result was fixations.

Freud also proposed a map of the mind dividing it into the conscious, the unconscious and the preconscious. There were three other parts to the mind – the ego, the rational self; the superego, which could be translated as the conscience; and the id, the most hedonistic of all. A British clinical psychologist I interviewed before he died gave one of the most entertaining descriptions of Freud's thinking. Freud saw the mind, Don Bannister wrote, as "basically a battlefield." The ego was in a dark cellar "in which a well-bred spinster lady (the superego) and a sex-crazed monkey (the id) are forever engaged in mortal combat, the struggle being refereed by a rather nervous bank clerk (the ego)."

The ego has to balance the demands of the id and the superego, which asks a great deal of a rather nervous bank clerk. Hergenjahn and Olson (2007) sum it up; "The id is the part of our mind we share with lower animals and is governed by the pleasure principle. The ego is the executive of the personality and is governed by the reality principle. The superego is the moral component of the personality and consists of the conscience and the ego ideal."

Freud said that the aim of psychoanalysis was as follows, that "Where id was, there ego shall be." The vampire's problem is that he or she is fixated at the oral stage.

The vampire has another psychological problem – sadism. No psychiatrist spoke of sadism till the nineteenth-century German, Richard von Krafft-Ebing. He named the natural tendencies to cruelty in honour of the eighteenth-century Marquis de Sade, who wrote;

> How delightful are the pleasures of the imagination! In those
> delectable moments, the whole world is ours; not a single creature

resists us, we devastate the world, we repopulate it with new objects which, in turn, we immolate. The means to every is ours, and we employ them all, we multiply the horror a hundredfold.
— Marquis de Sade, *Les prospérités du vice*

Poor sado de Sade spent much of his time in jail where he could not flog anyone, so he had to fantasize. It is astonishing that he had not attended an English public school. Winston Churchill once told the House of Commons that the beatings he received at his prep school were much worse than those inflicted on borstal boys. He was only removed from his prep school after the family doctor saw the marks on his bottom. George Orwell wrote a brilliant description of the beatings he received at school in *Such Were the Joys*. Orwell went to Eton, as Byron did. Polidori also went to a public school. They all knew about sadism, a factor in their vampire tales.

The vampire is not just an orally fixated sadist, but a cunning one. So he, or the rarer female sadist, seeks out masochists who hope to be beaten. Kraft-Ebbing named masochism after the nineteenth-century Leopold von Sacher-Masoch, author of *Venus in Furs*.

In *Three Papers on Sexual Theory*, Freud argued sadism and masochism are often found in the same individuals and called this sadomasochism. For him sadism was a distortion of the aggressive component of the male sexual instinct and masochism a form of sadism against the self.

The tendency to inflict and receive pain during intercourse was, Freud said, "the most common and important of all perversions," and ascribed it – as so much else – to incomplete or aberrant psychological development in early childhood.

As well as mapping the mind, Freud said famously that the baby was a polymorphous pervert. He had six children and observed them sporadically, though he hardly ever wrote about these observations. He was a fond father, however, and would have known that some 'normal' childhood behaviours include elements of sadomasochism. Tickling is the most benign. Freud's great hero Charles Darwin noted, back in 1837, that his baby son, William, laughed when tickled.

When Freud was developing his ideas, William Preyer (1895) got a baby to laugh by tickling when the child was only 8 weeks old. The British psychologist Valentine made his babies laugh by tickling them when they were just under 4 months old. In my Ph.D. thesis on the development of laughter, I suggested, not very originally, that tickling was a modified form of attack. Children like to be tickled but are also a little afraid of it.

Later, analysts Van der Bengh and Kelly wrote a review of the literature on vampires in 1964 and concluded:

> the popularity of the vampire figure evidences a role for Freud's notion of an inherent primary masochism. This erotic impulse is primitive in nature and seeming non-oedipal. Vampire dramatizations are a convenient location for the playing out of these repressed tensions.

Van der Bengh and Kelly stressed that drawing blood gave the vampire sexual pleasure and that:

> The specific symptoms of vampirism have their dynamic basis not only in the unresolved conflicts at the oral sadistic level, but at other levels of libidinal development as well. . . . Oedipal wishes, fear of castration, and aggressive hostile wishes, are examples of these many various unresolved conflicts which can be symbolized in the patients' minds by the blood.

The sadist may also want unconsciously to punish someone who attracts him precisely because they arouse his desire. We speak of sexual conquests, but the phrase is two-edged. I may conquer you by persuading you to sleep with me, but by making me want you, in some sense, you have also conquered me. The love object for the vampire is all object, however, just a trophy, a human tiger skin. Love does not come into it.

The original producer of True Blood, Alan Ball, summed up the popular appeal of vampires much more simply, as he said vampires *are* sex. I could argue that he got it only half right and should have said vampires are about sex – and more sex.

Freud's loyal biographer, Ernest Jones, wrote a long paper, On the Nightmare; he devoted 30 pages to the psychology of the vampire.

Vampires were versatile, Jones pointed out; they could change into animals – into cats in Japan and into pigs in Serbia, for instance. They often appeared as snakes. Odder than snakes, Jones pointed out, vampires can flit in the shape of charming butterflies. He didn't explain how butterflies bite. In some folk tales, vampires also sucked the udders of cows and goats. Milk and blood, the liquids of life.

Jones was the first psychoanalyst to explore in detail the relationship between vampires and the lure of death, "the land of mysterious possibilities, the land where all fantasies might be fulfilled" and "all secrets revealed." Death was not the end. We might never be truly posthumous if we had made sure our teeth were sharp and we found toothsome necks. As I warned at the beginning, vampires need to be studied seriously but also with some humour.

Jones had some vampire traits himself; he was sacked by two London hospitals for molesting women patients, though he drew the line at biting them. Freud, Jones and many psychoanalysts also believed fairy tales offered a window into the unconscious.

Freud's rival, Carl Jung, saw the vampire as representative of "the dark, unconscious aspect of the self that the ego tries to avoid as it bubbles with destructive energy." Jung developed the theory of the archetypes, figures that are ancient in the human psyche. The Healer archetype is intriguing and appears in every culture, from the earliest tribes of ancient man. It is a part of the human experience to be hurt, wounded or injured in some way, whether it be physical, emotional or spiritual. And because of this, there has always been someone who shows an aptitude for how to help the hurt person. The development of this archetype has had some interesting twists and turns in its very long life. Especially relevant to the vampire is the archetype of the Wounded Healer. Shamans have to be initiated and deliberately suffer pain before they can heal.

Some authors, such as Andrea Schneider, have suggested the vampire suffers from narcissism and is so self-centred he or she has no sympathy or empathy. Schneider has even coined the term narcissistic abuse. The only world is his own world. Narcissists will drain everyone else of ideas, energy, even blood, to feed their own needs.

From the 1890s, psychologists who were not Freudians also studied children's fears, as the great late-nineteenth-century English psychologist James Sully did. Children's fears were predictable; often they were afraid of the dark, and particularly of being left alone in the dark. They also were scared of animals, such as large barking dogs. Some children also feared fires, high places or thunderstorms. In the dark, monsters are especially terrifying. The main character in *Monsters, Inc.* is appropriately named after Sully. A factory which produces creatures that will scare children is at the heart of the action.

Both J. K. Rowling and, before her, J.R.R. Tolkien created memorable monsters – Voldemort who cannot be named and the legions of orcs Sauron commands. Tolkien taught Old English at Oxford and was very well read, so it is reasonable to suppose he had read some psychoanalytic material. In 1939, after he had finished *The Hobbit*, he gave a lecture on fairy stories, which he clearly thought important. He said, "It is a deeply perceptive commentary on the interdependence of language and human consciousness." He stressed it was not just for children.

In "On Fairy Stories," Tolkien distinguished them from 'traveller's tales', science fiction, beast tales and dream stories like *Alice in Wonderland*. The true fairy tale, he said, must be credible. "It is at any rate essential to a genuine fairy-story, as distinct from the employment of this form for lesser or debased purposes, that it should be presented as 'true'." But convincing.

Tolkien emphasized that through the use of fantasy, the reader could experience a rational and consistent world whose rules differed from those of the normal world. They had been an influence on him, as he said: "It was in fairy stories that I first divined the potency of the words, and the wonder of things, such as stone, and wood, and iron; tree and grass; house and fire; bread and wine." Fairy stories, he concluded, could provide moral or emotional consolation, through their happy ending, an ending children love. He emphasized the joy of the resolution. This echoes Freud's analysis of a satisfying joke. Tolkien concluded:

> Far more powerful and poignant is the effect [of joy] in a serious tale of Faerie. In such stories, when the sudden turn comes, we get a piercing glimpse of joy, and heart's desire, that for a moment passes outside the frame, rends indeed the very web of story, and lets a gleam come through.

Rowling's chronicles of Harry Potter often threaten an unhappy ending, but good eventually triumphs. Vampire tales are a darker fantasy, and usually climax – the pun is deliberate – in blood.

After Freud and Jones, another analyst, Bruno Bettelheim, studied fairy tales, which he saw as helpful in child development. In *Once Upon a Time*, Marina Warner includes 'On the Couch', a chapter in which she acknowledges the relevance of psychoanalysis for fairy tales and of Bettelheim's study, *The Uses of Enchantment* (1971). She gave her chapter on his work a title she took from an Angela Carter story 'House training the Id'. This is specifically what the parents of vampires never have done.

Current children's books do not have many vampires. An exception is *Vampire Baby* by Kelly and Meisel. When she starts teething, it's obvious she is not a normal baby. She sinks her pointy fangs into everything – furniture, toys and especially her big brother ("Youch, Tootie! No bite!"). Mom insists that it's just a phase, but Tootie's brother knows better and says "Just look at her hairline! Or the fact that all her favourite foods are blood red!" There is also the life-affirming *Little Vampire*, who is more interested in making friends than blood. There is also a Horrid Henry book for slightly older children in which Henry has to confront the Zombie Vampire. *Dracula Madness* brings in a dog detective, who sniffs out a man called McIver who never goes outside, never turns on his light and has bats flapping in his house. Dog versus vampire is, of course, cute rather than terrifying.

More recently, psychoanalysts have returned to the theme. For example, Van den Bergh and Kelly argued in 1964;

> The myth can be understood along various levels of psychosexual development: in oedipal terms, for example, the vampire is seen as an abductor of women, killing and enslaving any men who cross his path. . . . The significance and universal persistence of the myth suggests deep roots in the evolution of our psyche. It suggests the omnipresent desire to conquer the secret of life while containing the elements of its renewal. It represents the terrible desire for survival, destroying others to maintain his own existence. . . . Vampirism, as a mortal sin, is contained in the image that most often comes to mind, the perverse of the vampiric act, in which the bite and the sucking of blood produce an orgasmic sensation which supercedes coitus.

There are some interesting recent case histories too. Jolene Oppawasky (2011), who has written in detail on sexual abuse, has described a case of a 36-year-old man who reported sharing blood between five other adult men who also considered themselves to be vampires. After becoming engaged to a woman, the man entered therapy highly motivated to stop this behaviour. He stopped drinking blood altogether after two months.

Psychoanalysis offered a theory of how sadism developed – a key aspect of vampire psychology. Freud would have insisted, of course, that one had to examine Polidori's childhood to understand how he came to write *The Vampyre*.

4

THE DOCTOR WHO WANTED TO BE SOMETHING DIFFERENT

Poor Polidori came from an impressive family. His grandfather wrote a treatise on bones which was much admired, both for its scientific content and because it was written in verse. His uncle Luigi wrote a thesis on sleepwalking, which would influence Polidori. His father, Gaetano, was the secretary to a bad-tempered writer of tragedies, Count Vittorio Alfieri. The count was once compared to Dante in Italy, but now he is forgotten. Four years with the angry tragedian were enough for his secretary.

In 1790, Gaetano escaped to England, where he made a good living as a teacher of Italian – and as a translator of *Paradise Lost* and Horace Walpole's *The Castle of Otranto*, among many other works. In 1793, he married a governess, Anna Maria Pierce, whose father had run a successful business and left enough money for her husband to start a small publishing business. The couple had four sons and four daughters. John Polidori was born in 1795. All his life he would have to try to cope with Gaetano's ambitions and disappointments.

The boy was restless, Gaetano wrote, as "not doing anything was a great torment for him and when he happened to be inactive, he would have a strong expression tending to anger." Being very intelligent did not often help Polidori cope with his angers.

When he was 8, Polidori got into 'bad company'. Gaetano decided to send him to Ampleforth College, the now famous Catholic school. There were only 12 pupils, so the monks should have been able to ensure there was good discipline and minimal temptations. The letters between father and son reveals mutual anxiety, however. Gaetano expected his son to shine, and Polidori was always worried that he was disappointing his father.

Gaetano had already decided his son should study medicine even though the boy was not keen. Polidori voiced his objections cannily; "But do you not think I should be exposed to very great danger of having my morals corrupted by bad example?" University students were 'dissolute young men'. It might be dangerous to "expose me while young to their infectious society?" The dissolute young men were sometimes buying corpses which had been disinterred, as it was illegal for medical schools to acquire bodies for dissection. Gaetano did not relent; his son was going to study medicine over his dead body, if necessary.

Polidori enrolled at Edinburgh University in 1812. His ambivalence about a medical career is clear in his *An Essay upon the Source of Positive Pleasure*, which he started a year after he left Edinburgh. He wrote that a man "will not tell you of the profession he was studying, being one he abhorred; [or] of the hankering he had after history, poetry and literature, while he was obliged to study mathematics, medicine, or theology" (39–45). He did not join the Medical Society and made few friends among the other students. He was, however, devoted to his landlady, Mrs McDowall.

In 1814, Polidori asked Gaetano's permission to leave university to fight for the independence of Italy. He waxed patriotic about "the cry of my country, which now calls me to arms." Gaetano could not fight for his native country, as "you have a family and a wife. I on the contrary am free. I have no ties save those of country and glory." It was not just the lure of Italy; Polidori pointed out: "My disposition is not that of the English. They are automatons!" Gaetano snapped back: "Return to your reason; and, if you will be mad, wait until I am dead." So Polidori returned to reason, and Edinburgh.

Edinburgh students had to pass two final oral examinations. Facing these tests, Polidori fretted. Eventually he mustered up the courage to write to Gaetano to say he was delaying taking the examinations because he was 'unprepared'. He did not dare explain why; he was devoting much time to writing poetry and to his first play, *Cajetan*. Polidori's verse is neither brilliant nor embarrassing. *Cajetan* is awful.

In the preface to his verse play, *Ximenes*, he wrote;

> Poetry is the relaxation he (the author) sought for while tracing his path through the unstable sands of metaphysics and medical theory . . . it (poetry) can be laid down when severer studies require attention and resumed when a vacant moment arrives.

Polidori admitted that he was writing, "for the love of fame and for the sake of asserting a rank above the herd." He was something of a snob, a characteristic his vampire would share.

Students at Edinburgh could choose their own topic for their thesis, which they had to write in Latin. Theses were often written by the students' 'grinders', a less-than-flattering name for private tutors who ground out dissertations for a small fee. Polidori did not need to pay a grinder, as his uncle had produced a study of sleepwalking, a study that would influence his nephew's vampire. Luigi Polidori had sent his "Narrative of Oneirodynia with Convulsions and Madness" to the Royal College of Medical Doctors in London in 1793. About a third of Polidori's thesis was copied directly from Luigi's work.

Polidori called his 36-page thesis "*Disputatio Medica Inauguralis, Quaedam de Morbo, Oneirodynia Dicto, Complectens*" ("Inaugural Medical Dissertation Concerning Certain Aspects of the Disease Called Oneirodynia"). The term *oneirodynia* came from two Greek words, *oneiros* (dream) and *odyne* (pain). So it meant nightmares. William Cullen, who had taught at Edinburgh in the previous century, extended its definition to include "inflamed or disturbed imagination during sleep."

By the end of the eighteenth century the gothic had become fashionable. In 1799, Charles Brockden Brown's *Edgar Huntly; or, Memoires of a SleepWalker* was a farrago of nonsense, which did not stop it being a great success. It starts under an elm tree where a body was found. A man is digging. The digger, Clithero, turns out to be digging in his sleep. Asleep or awake, he is not popular. Only his landlady likes him, but she has her own secret, an evil twin brother who committed murder. Before he could be hanged, he fled to sea and was never heard of again.

The evil twin, however, is not dead. He comes back to England, tries to kill himself and then flees back to America. There he picks up the habit of sleepwalking from the native Indians. You couldn't make it up, but Charles Brockden Brown did.

Sleepwalking fascinated the late eighteenth and early nineteenth century because it seemed linked to the work of Mesmer and Puységur. Polidori certainly knew of Mesmer's demonstrations, and his friend William Taylor was interested in sleepwalking – and may even have suffered from it himself. With an uncle who had written about the subject, a friend who studied it and the fashion for the exotic, it is no surprise Polidori was drawn to study sleep walking.

Polidori's thesis started by trying to define it and put this 'extremely obscure disease' into some historical context ('Somnambulism' 775). He added;

> If I might offer a definition of this disease, I would say it is the habit of doing something in sleep that is usually done by those who are awake.
>
> ('Somnambulism' 776)

Polidori had never seen anyone sleepwalk, but he mined the literature effectively. The sleepwalker could be very busy. Some patients talked about what they had done recently; others answered questions; some even wrote essays and poems. Some somnambulists became violent; they drew a sword, let off pistols and even hit well-meaning people who sat by their bedside. The sleepwalker could be a tippler and 'guzzle wine'. Polidori was, after all, reporting on patients in Bordeaux and Italy, where the locals were knee deep in claret and Chianti.

The philosopher Leibniz's ideas were also influential. Leibniz (1646–1716) is most famous now for the invention of calculus and his rivalry with his contemporary Isaac Newton. Leibniz had some neurological ideas as well as about the universe. He claimed the brain was always active, even when we were sleeping. "At every moment there is in us an infinity of perceptions," Leibniz wrote, "unaccompanied by awareness or reflection." It is no surprise Freud read him with great interest. There were also theological implications, and Polidori was always interested in theology. At a time when few doubted the existence of God, the idea that complex, higher brain functions might be automatic or unconscious called into question the very "existence of the soul, the necessity of God, and the integrity of the self." Cinema-goers who read Leibniz – we have no surveys to identify this elite group – will be intrigued that Greenberg (2008) suggests a link between The Matrix and Leibniz's monads.

Polidori noted that if sleepwalkers were questioned, they could recall what happened in their last episode, and yet when awake, they remembered nothing about it. The implications were remarkable. "The soul as it thinks and remembers appears to be doubled, with the intellect following one track when it is asleep, but the other when it is awake" ('Somnambulism' 777).

"Intoxication, overeating, food that produces gas, . . . study, use of opium, and everything that moves blood to the brain" were also associated, Polidori wrote. A wound to the head had

> at times induced oneirodynia. . . . Moreover, oneirodynia sometimes presents along with hysteria, epilepsy and other diseases that arise from an affliction of the brain. This demonstrates plainly that oneirodynia is produced from an internal brain lesion. Yet it is much more typical for no clear cause to appear.

> ('Somnambulism' 777)

The second section of Polidori's thesis was made up of two case studies. The first was a riveting history of a 10-year-old boy his uncle Luigi had seen. The boy's family had a history of epilepsy and headaches; he himself suffered from convulsive tremors and pain, and sometimes a complication, "a period of brief sleep and calm that would suddenly give way to chattering and gesticulating" ('Somnambulism' 778).

The boy was also hyperactive. He "jumps around, tells about things he's seen, things that were done or said both recently and a while ago." When a household servant tried to grab him, the boy "resisted, throwing a series of vigorous punches his way." He also removed a picture from the wall, kissed it,

> and wanted it to lie down with him, even tucking it in for bed. Then he got off his bed and began hitting everyone he came across with his pillow and his fists and walked around his bedroom but never bumped into a wall – not only that.

After this he slept on top of a chest, arranging the pillow he had been carrying around under his head ('Somnambulism' 779). Astonishingly, while he was sleeping, the boy could toss his hat in the air and catch it. It never occurred to anyone the boy might be hamming it up.

The boy's memory was paradoxical. While sleepwalking, he could remember his previous nocturnal episodes, but he could not recall his nightly antics when awake.

Polidori's second case study was witnessed by a future Archbishop of Bordeaux. As a student, the Archbishop-to-be observed a priest who wrote elegant speeches in his sleep. The priest was also aquatic and provides perhaps the only case study of sleep swimming. One night, he imagined he was rescuing a boy who was drowning in an icy river. The fearless priest threw himself out of his bed, imitated all the motions of a swimmer on the floor of his room and . . . then "strayed from his bed shaking and with chattering teeth, as if he had truly emerged from a river" ('Somnambulism' 782).

Polidori did not send a draft of his thesis to his father or to his uncle.

In May 1815, before his final medical examination, he wrote to his sister Frances, "ask Mama what I am to do if I am flunked." How would he deal with his father? So it was a nervous student who walked into the house of Dr Hope on May 31, 1815 at four in the afternoon. The next day Dr Hope, however, told him he had passed and done so "with the utmost satisfaction to all the professors." He just had to decide what to do after he had qualified. Finally, he chose to make for London.

The London medical establishment, however, did not welcome any doctor coming from the provinces, let alone from north of the border. Doctors were not allowed to practice in the city until they were 26 years old. A little defeated, Polidori went to Norwich at the suggestion of William Taylor, his sleepwalking friend. Norwich, which had been the site of the first British blood libel, was about to feature in vampire history again.

Polidori stayed with Sir William Jerningham and, through him, he got an introduction that changed his life and led to the creation of the vampire. Jerningham knew the Prince Regent's doctor, William Knighton, and arranged for Polidori to meet him. Knighton gave Polidori an introduction to Lord Byron, then the most famous poet in England. Famous and neurotic.

Byron thought he needed a personal full-time physician. He was moody and often gave way to "silent rages, moody sullenness and revenge." His biographers have sometimes linked this dark side of his personality to the fact that his right foot was deformed. He had had much painful medical treatment, which turned out to be useless.

Byron was also neurotic about his digestive system, which was not surprising as he took laxatives as well as laudanum all the time. Anthea Hayter's fine *Opium and the Romantic Imagination* examined its influence, but what is curious is that Polidori never mentioned laudanum in his account of their travels.

In 1816, the great poet was under great stress. His separation from his wife had caused a society scandal, and there were rumours he had an affair with his half-sister, Augusta Leigh. Byron also owed unmanageable amounts of money which he could not pay, even though his poems sold well.

Byron never allowed his debts to stop his plans. He offered Polidori the generous salary of £100 a year, which the young man happily accepted. The relationship between the two men would not be easy, however, as Byron was always the master as well as the patient – and Polidori always the servant as well as the doctor. Polidori had had a domineering father; now he also had a domineering patient who really needed a team of psychiatrists.

Which of them was the vampire, one might ask?

Both, I will argue. Both had many of the characteristics of psychic vampires, who suck out energy from others but do not suck blood. I will argue that neither Byron nor Polidori felt themselves to be psychic vampires, however. They were about to embark on what sometimes looks like a *folie à deux*, with more than some sexual undertones.

Lord Byron was too haughty to ever consider himself the people's poet, but he too had to cope with the nineteenth-century equivalent of paparazzi, as Princess Diana did. Fans stalked him sometimes, and the really intrusive used telescopes to catch a glimpse of him.

Gaetano knew the dangers of working for a great ego, as he had left Italy to get away from Alfieri. He begged his son not to accept Byron's offer, but it was too tempting. Polidori was going to travel with the most celebrated poet in England and be paid, not just as a physician but as an author. Byron's publisher, John Murray, seems to have offered him £500 for an account of the journey. Today that would be an advance of somewhere in the region of £600,000. The fantastic offer was not crazy, as Byron was Murray's most successful author. The poet's adventures were bound to fascinate the public.

Byron had already toyed with vampire themes himself. His poem *Giaour* (1813) is the story of a female slave who has something like the curse of vampirism placed on her. But it is quite tame. Necks stay intact. Byron just said that the evil one flew "like a demon of the night" and ravished the woman.

We know a good deal about the journey Byron and Polidori took because the young doctor began a private diary, almost certainly for publication. The manuscript eventually came into the possession of his sister Charlotte, who was a first-class prude. Her nephew, Michael William Rossetti, inherited it and noticed his pious aunt had cut out a number of 'peccant', or sinning, passages. Rossetti claimed to have a good memory for the best bodice-ripping episodes. (With Byron anywhere near bodices were liable to rip all the time.) Charlotte had cut out one passage: "As soon as he reached his room, Byron fell like a thunderbolt upon the chambermaid." He does not seem to have believed in foreplay.

Sister Prude also cut out an account of a visit to "some haunt of the local Venus Pandemos" who was also known as *Venus vulgivaga*. Her haunt, however, was only a raucous music hall where actresses performed rude songs in scanty costumes. Polidori, his editor Rossetti remembered, described the performance "without any verbal impropriety." Despite that, Charlotte didn't think it right to let it stand.

In April 1816 Byron and Polidori set off very early to avoid any bailiffs who had a warrant to seize the folly coach that Byron had commissioned. This lunacy on wheels was copied from the celebrated one of Napoleon's taken at Genappe. It had a bed, a library, "a plate-chest, and every apparatus for dining." The vanity vehicle cost Byron £500, which, of course, he did not pay. When the bailiffs got to Byron's house, he was already hoofing it to Dover to set sail across the Channel.

Ten months earlier Napoleon had been defeated at Waterloo. He had been exiled to St Helena, remote in the South Atlantic, but Europe was fretted. The Emperor might materialize in the middle of the ocean, summon a fleet and sail north for revenge. The Navy spent a fortune patrolling the waters around St Helena to stop Napoleon leaving. Bureaucracy thrived in Europe because of such fears. Polidori's diary often mentions problems with passports, customs officials, and police as well as the bailiffs.

On May 4, Byron and Polidori travelled to the battlefield. The site had degenerated into a tourist trap. In St. Jean, the village that gave the French name to the battle, they "were shown cuirasses, helms, buttons, swords, eagles and regiment-books." They bought many before going to the farmhouse at Hougoumont which decided the battle. Everything was destroyed except the chapel. Byron and Polidori were then shown the spot where Colonel Howard, "my friend's cousin, was buried before being carried to England."

When they left Hougoumont. Byron started singing "a Turkish song – myself silent, full gallop cantering over the field, the finest one imaginable for a battle."

When they got to their inn, "we found the coach was jogged; so much so that it would not allow us to put confidence in it." Byron refused, as usual, to pay. The coach maker called in a warrant officer, who failed to persuade the British 'milord' to cough up. They left the city with Byron owing even more money.

On May 8, the three others who would take part in the writing of the ghost stories at the Villa Diodati – Shelley, Mary Wollstonecraft and Clare Claremont – were in Paris. It took Shelley and the two women five days to reach the Jura mountains. They then had to weather a snow storm before reaching Geneva. This is the first mention of the atrocious weather that would have so many consequences. The group took rooms in the Hotel Dejean on the north side of the lake.

As he and Byron made their way south, Polidori was often unwell; he needed more looking after than his patient. On May 9, he "got up very bad in Cologne." He cheered up, however, when after breakfast they heard a band play.

By his own account, at least, Polidori was helping his patient. On May 11, he wrote to Byron's friend, John Hobhouse, that "Byron's health was greatly improved," both because he was under less stress and thanks to exercise and peace of mind. Polidori did not provide more details. His 'corps delabre' (the literal translation is 'clapped out body') was much better; this left little for medicine "to patch up. Byron blithely spent much of the day singing songs like 'Here's to you Tom Brown'."

Polidori was ill again on the night of May 13, suffering "dreadful headaches: ate some stewed apples; took some more magnesia and acid; had no effect; lay down; got up after two hours." Two days later in Carlsruhe, Polidori was sick again at the inn. "Took ipecac, and op. gr. 15. Headache, vertigo, tendency to fainting, etc. Magnesia and lemon acid – a little better" and then contradicted himself, adding "no effect." It seems Byron was stressing Polidori and making him ill. Why will perhaps become clear later.

Eventually they reached Lausanne on the shores of Lake Geneva. There they visited a bookseller, who showed Polidori "a collection of bad books for four louis." Polidori could never resist books and bought the bad books. The lake itself was disappointing, as it did not look very broad.

They travelled on to Secheron. At their hotel, Byron larked and put his age down as 100, which Polidori thought 'worthy of a novel'. Shelley, Mary Wollstonecraft and Byron's young mistress, Claire Claremont, had settled into the Hotel de L'Angleterre. They all met when Byron and Polidori arrived. The 'creators' were all assembled.

It was not likely to be an easy gathering. Shelley had some doubts about Byron's poetry. He felt Byron was "a slave to the vilest and most vulgar prejudices and as mad as the winds." There would be some conflicts between the two poets, who both had psychological flaws.

Byron had rented the Villa Diodati on the shore of Lake Geneva. It was a fine building with a fine history; it was built in the seventeenth century by John Diodati, a theologian. John Milton had visited him to discuss translations of the Bible.

By conventional standards the morals of the three men and two women were shocking. Shelley treated Mary Wollstonecraft Godwin as his wife, though they were not married, while Claire Claremont was the latest of Byron's many mistresses. Byron was bisexual. He had had crushes on fellow pupils at Eton and one very serious affair with John Edleston, a choirboy at Trinity Chapel. Byron himself was at Trinity from 1805 until June 1807.

In May 1807 he scribbled a note:

D – R – T [Dearest?] – Why not? With this kiss make me yours again forever.

Byron

As a pledge of their love, Edleston in 1806 gave Byron a cornelian brooch pin in the shape of a heart, to which Byron refers in his poem "The Adieu". In a series of poems Edleston is disguised under the feminine name 'Thyrza'. Several were suppressed after their initial publication. Byron asked his boyhood friend, Edward Noel Long: "pray, keep the subject of my 'Cornelian' a Secret." Thomas Moore, Byron's friend and first biographer, allowed Byron's memoir to be destroyed and excised the homosexual passages from the surviving journals and letters; it was certainly an example of the love that dared not speak its name. Byron called Edleston Byron's 'adopted brother' – a very tame tag given the passion of the poetry which referred to "the pressure of the thrilling hand" and "the kiss so guiltless and refin'd," so that even "passion blushed to plead for more."

Byron left England in 1809. His confidant John Hobhouse recorded in his diary on June 6, 1810: "messenger arrived from England – bringing a letter from [Francis] Hodgson to B[yron] – tales spread – the Edleston accused of indecency."

In Greece and Turkey in 1810 and 1811, Byron was not inhibited. He acquired a new companion, the teenager Nicolo Giraud, whom he made his principal beneficiary in his will. Byron returned to England – which he loathed because of its cant and puritanism – after the death of his mother in 1811, only to learn from Edleston's sister that his lover had died of consumption in May that year. Byron wrote seven elegies to his lover.

The sexual atmosphere at the villa understandably confused Polidori at times. He called Claire Clairmont the 'sister' of Mary Wollstonecraft Godwin and, for a while, he thought the two women were true sisters, but there was no blood-relationship. Mary was the daughter of Mr and the first Mrs Godwin, and Claire the daughter of Mr and Mrs Clairmont. Polidori, however, said nothing about Byron's penchant for beautiful young men.

Polidori said much more about Shelley, who he found, "bashful, shy, consumptive; twenty-six; separated from his wife; keeps the two daughters of Godwin, who practice his theories." Shelley lived according to these wild theories, Polidori believed that he was the lover of Claire Clairmont, as well as of Godwin's daughter, Mary Wollstonecraft Godwin.

Once Byron had installed himself at the Villa Diodati, there was much socializing and 'confabbing' as Polidori called it. One evening Shelley and Byron had "some very confidential talk." For Byron and Shelley, Polidori was not an equal. He was perhaps more than a servant, but still not really one of them, so it didn't matter what he heard.

Both famous poets had problematic childhoods. Byron's parents had an unhappy marriage; his father was nicknamed 'mad Jack'. The tensions at the Villa Diodati may have an added cause. Since his time as a pupil at Eton. Byron had had a number of crushes on young men, as we have seen. In Norwich, Harriett Martineau, one of Queen Victoria's favourite authors, had been struck by Polidori's beauty and his remarkable profile.

It is possible that Polidori had been ill on the way to Geneva because he feared Byron's advances. It must be said, though no surviving letters mention any such event. That is not surprising, as John Murray destroyed many of Byron's letters after Byron died. My suggestion is speculation, but it makes some psychological sense given Byron's history and his often erratic behaviour towards his young physician.

Byron had teased Polidori and once was a little violent towards him, but now he showed some kindness towards him. They went to a watchmaker, and the poet paid 15 napoleons towards a watch for Polidori. Given my speculation that Byron might have wanted to seduce him, was this a love gift?

If the group had been able to go out on the lake, literary history might have been different. There was a vineyard between the Villa Diodati and Shelley Cottage, and close to that, they moored one boat they now shared. On May 30, Polidori breakfasted with "Mr and Mrs Shelley (and) rowed out to see a house together. The next day they all rowed on the lake with Byron. I, Mrs Shelley, and Miss Godwin" (he meant Clare but got her surname wrong) till nine.

Everyone who would be involved at the creation of the vampire and Frankenstein was now in or around the Villa Diodati. There were no weather reports from afar, of course, in 1816, so they did not know that Mount Tamboro, a volcano in Indonesia, had just erupted.

It spewed clouds of ash into the atmosphere. The ash drifted towards Europe, ruining the summer with storms. It would soon be mad to try to row on the lake.

NOTE

1   Vanessa Grigoriadis, "The Joy of Vampire Sex: The Schlocky, Sensual Secrets Behind the Success of 'True Blood,'" *Rolling Stone*, June 10, 2011.

5

THE VAMPIRE DEVELOPS, ACADEMIC STUDIES AND THE POET FLEES THE BAILIFFS

Before describing how the first vampire tales came to be written, it seems useful to outline the main characteristics of vampires and when they first appeared.

Supernaturally strong – dates from antiquity.

Supernaturally vain – the sixteenth-century Elizabeth Bathory was certainly that.

Hypnotist – 1816, as Polidori's vampire hypnotizes the women he wants to seduce.

Seductive – until Byron and Polidori wrote, the only seductive vampires seem to have been women. In Jewish lore Lilith took many human lovers as well as turning good angels into her bed. Elizabeth Bathory rarely denied herself a fanciable girl.

Utterly evil – dates from antiquity. Lilith was that.

Does not die – this was a feature that harks back at least to the graves that were dug up in the 1730s.

Monstrous teeth – these do not feature in the eighteenth-century legends. Mid-1850s.

Orally fixated – Freud's key contribution in 1909.

Cannot stand daylight – Polidori's story seems to have first attributed that to vampires.

Not reflected in mirrors – this was invented by Stoker in 1896.

Vulnerable to crosses – a mediaeval touch. Christ would protect someone who deployed a crucifix.

Vulnerable to the Mediterranean diet, as the vampire cannot stand garlic – Stoker added that culinary touch.

Able to read minds – that was first described by Polidori as a power the vampire had.

A love of silver – another invention of Stoker's in 1896.

The ability to fly and leap great distances – there seems to have been no mention of that utnil Anne Rice made Lestat fly after he had absorbed the blood of some ancient vampires. Then in the films of Twilight (2008–2012), the hero climbs trees faster than a lemur and flies carrying his girlfriend on his back. Twilight was using an effect that had been used in the Superman comics, in kung fu films and notably in Ang Lee's magnificent Crouching Tiger Hidden Dragon.

In need of therapy – in 1973 Anne Rice added that Freudian touch in her Interview with A Vampire.

The development of vampire characteristics oddly does not feature much in the recent field of academic studies which is usually called vampirology.

As I suggested at the start, one of the challenges for this book is to represent the growing discipline of vampire studies fairly. The claims it makes are sometimes a little strident. Many studies depend on self-reports, which are often not that reliable. One notable absence from the books and papers is the research on cults. The literature suggests that many individuals are drawn to cults as a result of damaging childhood experiences, poor parenting which makes them bad at relating to people, attachment disorder, a history of abuse or neglect, low self-esteem and a lack of close friends. Teenagers are likely to be very aware of these problems in themselves and so get recruited easily as they look for anchors for their being. Vampire studies offer little analysis of that or of the considerable research done on cults in the wake of tragedies.

The Jonestown massacre in 1978 culminated in 918 deaths after the killing of United States Congressman Leo Ryan and others as they tried to leave the compound. Those killings, along with the massacre, were ordered by the cult's charismatic leader, Jim Jones. Mark Lane, who had accompanied Ryan into Jonestown on a fact-finding mission, was held hostage during the massacre. "I will tell the world the truth about what happened here," he warned. Miraculously, the guards allowed him to escape. Lane's book examined the origins of the cult, analyzed the reasons for Ryan's investigation into the community and charted how Jim Jones became increasingly irrational and ordered the killings.

There have also been many analyses of the events at Waco in 1993 and the 94 deaths, which started a year later, in the Order of the Solar Temple. There were more strange deaths in 1995 in the Vercors, an isolated area of France, and then yet more in Canada two years later. Two films that I made with David Carr Brown found the Order was usual in one way: disciples believed they were privileged and were receiving esoteric secrets, as Thierry Huguenin described in his book, The 54th. The Solar Temple was unusual, however, because it attracted many immensely successful individuals. The groups at Jonestown and Waco included almost no one like that, except for the congressman. One key finding was common. Cults are secretive because they fear the real world, and they exhibit strong group loyalty. Some of the characteristics of cults are similar to those of vampire 'alliances', a term academics sometimes employ.

Jeanne Keyes Youngson, founded the Count Dracula Fan Club in 1965. It started as an organization dedicated to Dracula and vampire fiction and film, but she began to get letters from individuals who said they were real vampires. She followed these up, which was not always easy, as vampires tended to be secretive. In 1972, Stephen Kaplan formed the Vampire Research Centre in Suffolk County, New York. He supervised a 'vampire hotline', which received numerous phone calls (many of them hoaxes) from real vampires.

In 1977, the Vampire Studies Society started to print a quarterly newsletter titled Journal of Vampirism. It was not a learned journal, as it mainly offered vampires the chance to explain themselves. It only lasted five years. In 1978 Kaplan started the Vampire Information

Exchange, which published through to the mid-2000s the *Vampire Information Exchange Newsletter*. The 1990s also saw a number of Anne Rice conventions, which allowed vampires to meet and presumably interview each other.

The 2000s saw vampires find their voices, as some of them turned academic. Among the best known in what does remain a niche area are Michelle Belanger, the exotically named Corvis Nocturnum – Corvis was the king of Hungary who threatened Vlad the Impaler – and Merticus of the Atlanta Vampire Alliance, which has published a massive survey of 379 questions to which some 950 self-identified vampires responded.

Academic vampires like Belanger usually describe themselves as psychic vampires. Her *The Psychic Vampire Codex: A Manual of Magick and Energy Work* examines the daily life of the 'vampire community'. She distinguishes between psychic and sanguinarian vampires. The first do not drink blood but suck out other people's energy, which is why they are called psychic. The sanguinarians, as the term implies, drink blood. As we shall see, however, contemporary vampires do not bite necks of unwilling victims but take blood from donors who know and may even like what is being done to them. The process has become rather medicalized and hygienic, as they usually use syringes to draw the blood. Finally, *Vampires in Their Own Words: An Anthology of Vampire Voices* is a compilation of personal narratives.

To meet any subjects at all, researchers must get access to the 'vampire community'. As they develop contacts and relationships, they risk becoming advocates rather than dispassionate researchers, that ideal but elusive scientific type.

Laycock's *Vampires Today: The Truth about Modern Vampirism* uses interviews with members of the Atlanta Vampires Alliance. He argues that

> vampirism should be viewed foremost as an identity around which social and religious institutions have formed. This model accounts for the mosaic of religious and cultural orientations held by vampires and acknowledges the vampire community's claims that vampirism is not a choice. It also facilitates a

functionalist reading of vampire discourse as validating a new category of person.

The final sentence, which claims that "vampire discourse" somehow makes for "a new category of person," is an ambitious claim that would make many academic psychologists pause. One does not conjure up new categories of being lightly, but Laycock does not hesitate and also introduces the concept of 'otherkins', "individuals who identify as 'not entirely human'."

Otherkins have an unorthodox "framework of metaphysical beliefs," Laycock says, "If it were orthodox they would not be otherkin." Laycock develops a grand theory that "the Otherkin community serves existential and social functions commonly associated with religion. In the final analysis, the Otherkin community is regarded as an alternative nomos – a socially constructed worldview – that sustains alternate ontologies." In other words, they see themselves as not quite like us. And we don't see them as much like us, though we like going to the movies to see what they do.

Williams and Browning are less metaphysical. Browning estimates there are over 5,000 vampires in the United States. The Atlanta Vampire Alliance is more bullish and suggests there are nearly that number in Atlanta itself. But the numbers may have peaked. The Alliance frets that 'real vampires' might prove to be a fad of sorts but is pleased that few vampires seem to want to be cured. Only 8% of those who responded to the survey stated that they would "permanently end their vampiric condition and instead live a normal life" if given the chance. The Alliance and Browning both present vampires as normal people who have jobs and families, go shopping and watch movies. Drinking blood is a ritual they fit into recognizable ordinary lives – and their only striking oddity.

Some vampires do admit they have had enough, however. Browning reported that Alexia told him: "If the cause could be identified, I would most certainly take a pharmaceutical pill."

Williams and Browning developed open-ended questionnaires. They found that most of those they studied "were distrustful of social workers and helping professionals and preferred to 'stay in the coffin' for fear of being misunderstood, labelled and potentially having to face severe repercussions to their lives."

The question of whether vampirism is a fetish is interesting. Williams compares them to individuals with "'divergent sexual identities' who engage in bondage-discipline/dominance-submission/ sadomasochism." Williams and Emily Prior, the executive director of the Centre for Positive Sexuality, also stress 'real vampires' often have considerable fear about 'coming out of the coffin'. They argue that social workers and other helping professionals have to remember that those who espouse vampire identities are

> people – they have common issues like those with mainstream identities . . . [and] are fearful that clinicians will label them as being psychopathological in some way (i.e., delusional, immature, unstable), perhaps wicked, and not competent to perform in typical social roles, such as parenting.

Social workers and others, Williams and Prior say:

> should learn more about alternative identities and communities, listen and learn from clients, strive to become more aware of our own potential biases and stereotypes, and interrogate and challenge common social discourses that pathologize and demonize. By doing so, social workers can establish trust with clients who have alternative identities and belief systems, provide services to a more diverse clientele, and establish strong alliances that contribute to effective service.

This advice is sensible, but the authors are as much advocates as researchers. This does not mean one should ignore their work, but one should be aware of a certain bias.

Though he too is sympathetic, Browning is a little more objective. He has admitted that "Until 2009, the only area of vampire studies that I hadn't approached was real vampires." He had been studying the vampire in films and literature. "I think I subconsciously saved it for last because I just thought what a lot of people think: that they must be crazy and have read too much fictional work about vampires."

In his search, Browning went to New Orleans. He was talking to the store owner of Wicked Orleans, a Gothic-style clothing and leather shop in the French Quarter, when a middle-aged woman and two teenage boys walked through the door.

The store owner stopped mid-sentence. This woman was one of the people Browning was looking for. He approached her and started talking to her about his ethnographic study of 'real vampires'. Did she know anyone who fit that description?

The woman smiled, and Browning had his answer – her open lips revealed teeth that had been filed to a point, like fangs.

A few weeks later, Browning met an 'elder vampire' who invited him to meetings of the New Orleans Vampire Association. Browning discovered that there were about 50 vampires living in New Orleans alone. "After a short period of time," he said, "I realized that they weren't crazy. At least, they weren't any crazier than your Average Joe."

The Average Joe, however, does not want to drink blood. No one is certain what causes haematomania, the craving to drink blood, but it is likely to be a mixture of physical and psychological causes. In Chapter 13, I examine the evidence for what may cause the craving, according to perhaps more objective studies. Browning found that those who experience the need describe it as an intense thirst-like sensation. They compared it to an addiction with withdrawal-like symptoms. Animal blood or rare steaks may act as substitutes, but for most vampires nothing beats fresh blood. Horror films sometimes give the impression that a vampire needs tumblers of blood every day. For many a few teaspoons once a week is enough, Browning learned.

The craving can be acute. When a vampire called Kinesia went four months without feeding, she found herself in the emergency room with a low heart rate that would shoot up to 160 when she stood up or walked around. When she was bloodless, as it were, she suffered massive migraines and sometimes even lost consciousness. He also reported the case of a woman who found herself unable to go to work or even walk after a period of not ingesting blood. When her husband came to see her in the hospital, she fed from him in her room and immediately felt better.

Browning and others compare becoming a vampire to realizing one is gay. The moment a person first felt they were a vampire was rarely a 'eureka' moment. Symptoms started to surface around puberty, often when teenagers felt themselves physically 'drained' and could not begin to explain why. They often discovered accidentally that blood was a tonic; a teenager might bite his or her lip, for instance. He or she realizes that swallowing the blood provides instant energy. The movies have got that wrong time and again. Most vampires are not converted by one bite. For most, it's a gradual and frightening process, which sometimes happens in puberty – sex again – or possibly after a trauma.

Thomas Miller (2008) suggested a link with games like Dungeons and Dragons, saying rather dramatically that these pretences turned into "games and rituals that include bloodletting, sacrifice, group sex and drugs in which membership engage." They added; "For some, bloodletting and sexually perverse activities are the ultimate sexual experience. It is a means of intimate communication with another person, which has been lacking in their family and peer experiences."

I have not done field research the way Browning has done, but in the course of writing this book I met an architect called Amanda who is now 25 years old. She told me how vampires fascinated her when she was a teenager. She wanted to be one. She suspected now that her fascination was linked to her anxieties about sex. They were very strong, and she remembered her fascination with some fondness. As she grew up and sex became less of mystery, she grew out of it, however. It had been a teenage phase – and craze.

The subjects Browning interviewed ranged in age from 18–50. He was astonished by how normal they seemed. They described themselves as atheistic, monotheistic or polytheistic; self-identified as heterosexual, homosexual and bisexual; some were parents; married and divorced; Some were wearing or have worn fangs, or had, or have had, naturally long incisors. Nearly all seemed to be competent citizens, and said that they performed bloodletting and other similar rituals safely and did so only with willing donors. They went regularly for medical check-ups that hardly ever revealed complications as a result of their feeding practices.

The Atlanta Vampire Alliance is clear that

> vampires are generally individuals who cannot adequately sustain their own physical, mental, or spiritual well-being without the taking of blood or vital life force energy from other sources; often human. Without feeding the vampire will become lethargic, sickly, depressed and often go through physical suffering or discomfort.

They did not report extreme levels of distress. According to the Atlanta Vampire Alliance research, 17% suffered from anaemia and 20% from chronic fatigue syndrome; 31% had had a psychiatric episode, which is not very different from the incidence reported in 'normal' populations. Statistics claim that one in four of us will have some such episode. None had, or admitted to, a conviction for a serious crime.

These unexceptional citizens were still anxious. They did not march in 'proud to be a vampire' parades, similar to the 'proud to be gay' parades. Most of those Browning interviewed hesitated to 'come out'. Being gay himself, he understands that anxiety. The vampires were largely determined to keep what they were secret. Yet there is also a certain arrogance as "Vampires often display signs of empathy, sense emotions, perceive auras, and are generally psychically aware of the world around them," according to the Atlanta Vampire Alliance, although they do not claim to be a "new category of person."

Secret societies tend to have their own jargon – and Browning found that was true of the 'vampire community'. To 'feed' is to drink blood, while those who give their blood are called 'donors'. Being 'awakened' and 'coming out of the coffin' are ways to talk about becoming aware of one's vampiric identity.

Not every vampire drinks blood, as stated. Some simply get strength from taking the 'psychic energy' of others. One of the most disturbing findings perhaps that Browning provides suggests giving someone a massage may do the trick and allow a psychic vampire to steal their energies. The Atlantic Vampire Alliance also boasts that both blood drinkers and psychic vampires "may display various levels of psychic ability." Again, however, the literature does not examine links with the extensive – if never conclusive – literature on parapsychology. A brief history may be helpful.

In 1853, the chemist Robert Hare conducted experiments with mediums and reported positive results, but his results were soon criticized for lack of rigour. Over five months, also in 1853, a French politician began to dabble in the occult. Agenor de Gasparin conducted early experiments into table-tipping. Again, critics suspected trickery, because those sitting at the table might have been to joggle it with their knees and no one took the precaution of looking under the table. There were studies of telepathy, hauntings, ectoplasm and much else that science could not explain. One of the most interesting studies was the 1894 *Census of Hallucinations*, which sampled 17,000 people. Out of these, 1,684 persons admitted to having experienced a hallucination or an apparition, which suggests there was some audience ready to believe in occult phenomena.

In 1911, Stanford University became the first academic institution in the United States to study extrasensory perception (ESP) and psychokinesis, the moving of objects without touching them. in a laboratory setting. The psychologist William MacDougall, whose work on instincts was useful, then encouraged a young psychologist, J.B Rhine, to develop a more quantitative approach. He used cards and dice to see if one subject could know whether another subject, isolated in a different room, could know what the first subject was seeing. Rhine told me in 1976 that he prided himself on the fact that one could replicate his experiments. Rhine also started the *Journal of Parapsychology*, which he co-edited with McDougall. Rhine said in 1934 that after 90,000 trials, he felt ESP is "an actual and demonstrable occurrence."

I also interviewed the marine biologist Sir Alistair Hardy, who is famous for mapping the distribution of plankton in the ocean. He

co-wrote *The Challenge of Chance* and backed the setting up of an insti-
tute to study religious experiences and parapsychology. Vampires
never came up in my interviews. The academics who discuss vampirism seem rather unaware of these paranormal studies, however.
Rhine was later dismayed to find that one of his students had faked
some results.

One year into his study, Browning tried being a donor himself
at a charity event, where community-minded vampires provided
food for the homeless. He discovered that each vampire had his or
her particular method of taking blood. The person who blooded
him used a disposable scalpel to make a tiny prick on his back, and
then used his fingers to squeeze the area until blood came out. He
put his mouth on the wound and lapped up the blood. He repeated
the process two or three times before cleaning the wound. The
pricking hurt, but mostly because he's a 'needle-phobe', Browning said.

In a classic 1970 study "The Gift Relationship: From Human Blood
to Social Policy," Richard Titmuss compared the voluntary British system of giving blood favourably with the American one, in which
payments were then widely made. He reckoned such a market was
inefficient and wasteful, that it created shortages and surpluses, and
led eventually to a contaminated product.

Vampires take blood, but researchers again do not mention
research on donors to blood banks, though the subject is relevant
and continues to be studied by sociologists. For example, a recent
Brazilian study of 20 donors and 20 recipients found that giving
blood was very positive – for obvious reasons for those who received
blood but for very similar ones for those who donated. In Brazil,
donors are not paid.

The study gathered a number of witness statements from which it
quoted. Their simplicity is worth noting;

> Donating means cooperating with life, with the facility (blood
> bank), helping others and oneself, because we have the right
> to exams every three months, so helping others not expecting

anything in return; in addition to having the right to take the day off, though I never do.

(Lucas)

Helping others. People need it and one day I may need it, so I need to do my share to ensure I'll have it. I need to help somehow whoever is in need. I always had a desire to help, perhaps because of my upbringing.

(Marcos)

Donating life, because giving blood helps people live, like when there're accidents. As when my grandma got ill and needed several blood transfusions and it helped her to stay longer with us, before she died. . . . Giving a little blood you won't miss, can save lives.

(Felipe)

It's an act of solidarity because I guess that people who donate are more humane than those who receive it. I guess that donors are very important for me. I guess they should take care of themselves because they save lives and because of them I'm here today; they prolonged my life.

(Emanuele)

Usually altruism is less of a factor in vampire blood exchange, though Browning found friends would do it for each other. Show me yours and I'll show you mine. Blood was given for blood money. People let themselves be bled for payment and, sometimes, even for sexual favours. Browning seems surprisingly disappointed by that, given his original research was on vampire movies and novels, genres where altruism does not feature much. Vampires approach these potential donors, he also found, only after having observed them for some time and only if they are fairly certain they are unlikely to 'freak out'.

The need for blood may be psychological, according to Tomas Ganz, a medical doctor and professor at UCLA;

> There is likely a strong placebo effect, akin to ingesting bitter powders, brightly coloured liquids or other substances that do not look or taste like conventional foods. This effect can be further enhanced if there is a ritual component associated with the ingestion, and if the individual feels a sense of some kind of exclusivity (such as drinking a very expensive and rare wine).

Browning learned that some vampires claim they can't control their urges and need two or three feedings a week. If there is blood a-plenty, they may refrigerate it. Later they may combine it with other ingredients. For its part the Atlanta Vampire Alliance insists vampires eat normally. "Most people are able to maintain healthy energy levels through diet, exercise, social interactions and the occasional cappuccino," says Merticus, who is one of the voices of the vampire community "We've had to develop alternative means to sate our energy needs." No vampire seems to be a vegan. Most vampires do not confide in their doctors because they are wary of stigma.

Merticus at least is not grandiose. "We do not identify with fictional characters, supernatural powers, or immortality, nor do we have any difficulty distinguishing between fantasy and reality," he says, adding that if anything, pop culture is catching up to them.

As there is no 'test' for vampirism, the Alliance welcomes anyone. Members apparently include doctors, lawyers, soldiers, scientists, soldiers, artists, teachers and parents of every age, gender, ethnicity and religion.

Browning argues the vampires are doing good, "because it helps put into perspective what our conception of 'normal' is." Their actions are not the problem; our reactions are. "It's our preconceived notion of what normal is that's the problem," Browning insists.

When Browning started his research, he was surprised that most of the community members knew little of the way vampires are portrayed in popular culture. Once, when he mentioned an episode of the TV series *True Blood*, he said, "no one knew what I was talking about." The vampires weren't super-fans whose obsession with fantasy had spiralled to an extreme. Rather, they were normal people with routines no different from everyone else.

In Britain, there was much activity around the centenary of Stoker's death in 2012. Most of it was literary rather than psychological. Dacre Stoker, the great-grand-nephew of Bram and author of *Dracula: The Un-Dead* gave a lecture.

Delegates visited the Golders Green Crematorium to pay their respects to Stoker. Marx and Freud also are buried in Golders Green, as well as Marc Bolan, whose song "I'm Just a Vampire for Your Love" ignores the fact that real vampires don't often do love.

Sam George of the University of Hertfordshire offers a series of workshops which cover the psychology, literature, and politics of vampires and much else. As they make clear the ambition of vampire-ology, it is necessary to analyse what the workshops offer in a little detail.

They open with the arrival of the Romantic Byronic vampire "and interrogate differing perspectives on the textual relationship between Byron and Polidori. Byron as a real life model for this new aristocratic vampire is also investigated alongside issues of nationality and social class." After a workshop on melodrama, it is on to Marx and the vampire as capitalist.

Sex is of the essence, especially deviant sex, with a discussion of Christopher Craft's "Kiss Me with Those Red Lips." George compares Stoker and Wilde. Then the TV personality Gyles Brandreth wrote *Oscar Wilde and the Vampire Murders*. The novel opens in 1890 at a glamorous party given by the Duke and Duchess of Albemarle. Even the Prince of Wales is there. Wilde is interested in a less pot-bellied guest, Rex LaSalle, a young actor who claims to be a vampire. The Duchess is found murdered – with two tiny puncture marks on her throat. The Prince asks Oscar and his friend Arthur Conan Doyle to investigate. The denouement need not detain us.

In real life, the true vampires were, of course, Wilde's lover, Lord Alfred Douglas, and his father, who left the note that Wilde was posing as a sodomite. Both sucked the life out of the great writer. He was sentenced to jail, spent two years in Reading Jail and was only 46 when he died. Who knows what he might have written if he had not died so young?

The workshops then move on Anne Rice, whose *Interview with a Vampire* led the vampire onto the analytic couch. The workshops also discuss the vampire's less charismatic cousins, the zombies, who do not hunger for blood but corpses, which they like to eat. The vampire is far too well-mannered to be a cannibal, while the zombie is no English gentleman. The word is of Haitian origin and linked to voodoo. The Oxford English Dictionary argues zombies came from the West African Kongo words *nzambi* (god) and *zumbi* (fetish). It was first recorded in 1819, in a history of Brazil by the poet Robert Southey. There is here an insinuation which supports my speculation that Byron had designs on Polidori. Southey suggested Byron and Southey were 'in a league of incest', so some sex may be inferred.

Zombies feature in what is sometimes reckoned to be the worst film ever made, the so-bad-it's-marvellous *Plan 9 from Outer Space* (1959). The workshops advertise that they will discuss the zombie "within debates around identity politics and difference." The last prospectus for the workshops does not mention *Abraham Lincoln: Vampire Hunter*, which is analysed in the last chapter.

Dr Sam George finishes her workshops with "A Return to Folklore and Confronting Death in Young Adult Vampire Fiction." Her work signals the arrival of a niche discipline which, as she acknowledges, owes much to Polidori and the psychodramas at the Villa Diodati.

6

DIP THE PEN IN BLOOD

The vampire stories were far from peaceful and written in a far from peaceful atmosphere. In 1816, once Byron, Polidori, Shelley, Mary Wollstonecraft and Claire Claremont were established at the Villa Diodati and the small house nearby, they got into a routine of soirees and rowing. At the start of June, Polidori was boating on the lake with Shelley and Byron, "who quarrelled with me." Polidori was jealous of Shelley, and Shelley's biographer, Dowden, said that "on one occasion, suffering from the cruel wrong of having been a loser in a sailing-match, he went so far as to send Shelley a challenge, which was received with a fit of becoming laughter."

Byron was more menacing and told his physician that, "though Shelley has some scruples about duelling, I have none and shall be at all times ready to take his place." Polidori soon gave him reason, as he hit Byron's knee with an oar while they were rowing. Was Byron trying to play footsie? We do not know.

The lake was often rough. In one letter to Murray, Byron described a stormy night in which Shelley, who could not swim, kept his calm when the boat seemed about to capsize and refused Byron's offer to save him should he fall in the water.

The evening of June 14, two nights before Byron started the game of writing supernatural stories, was social. Polidori went to yet another soiree where they discussed somnambulism. The next day, he was clumsy again. It's a blessing he never worked as a surgeon. After dinner, he had another accident which was, in some sense, Byron's fault. It had rained and Mary Shelley was walking up the hill to Diodati. Byron saw her from his balcony where he was standing with Polidori and said to him: "Now you who wish to be gallant ought to jump down this small height and offer your arm." Polidori tried but, on the wet ground, his foot slipped and he sprained his ankle. Byron helped carry him into the villa, put him on the sofa and went upstairs to fetch a pillow for him. Polidori was sulky and said to Byron; "Well, I did not believe you had so much feeling." The injury, Byron wrote to John Murray, was serious, as Polidori had to be taken to hospital. Byron concluded that "he can't jump."

Polidori could not write plays any more than he could jump, as the group saw. When Shelley came to the villa in the evening, they discussed *Cajetan*, "which all agreed was worth nothing." After his drama had been mangled, Polidori said; "Shelley and I had a conversation about principles – whether man was to be thought merely an instrument." The word 'instrument' needs some explanation. In 1764, the French philosopher La Mettrie had published a book which claimed man was just a machine, with no soul. The key point is that machines could be manufactured, and if human beings were machines, they too could be manufactured. The Golem, the creature imagined by a rabbi in Prague, was supposed to help the Jews of that city because they needed a giant to protect them.

This conversation, Michael Rossetti wrote, appeared to be similar to one Mary Shelley had, "which raised in her mind a train of thought conducing to her invention of Frankenstein and his Man-monster."

What was the nature, they questioned, "of the principle of life? Would it ever be discovered?" Then they moved on to crux of the matter; would "the power of communicating life be acquired? Perhaps a corpse would be reanimated; galvanism had given token of such things."

Galvanism was named after Luigi Galvani (1737–1798), who investigated the effect of electricity on dissected animals. Scientists respected his theory, and Galvani is seen now as an important pioneer in biology. In 1786 he discovered that when a frog's legs are touched by both a copper probe and a piece of iron at the same time, then they twitch just as if an electric current were present. We know now that even the brain depends on electro-chemical charges.

That night Mary Shelley did not sleep, perhaps because the idea for Frankenstein was forming in her mind. She did eventually record the dream which inspired her book.

> I saw the pale student of unhallowed arts kneeling beside the thing he had put together. I saw the hideous phantasm of a man stretched out, and then, on the working of some powerful engine, show signs of life, and stir with an uneasy, half vital motion.

She experienced 'a thrill of fear'. She wanted to

> forget my hideous phantom; still it haunted me. I must try to think of something else. I recurred to my ghost story, my tiresome unlucky ghost story! O! if I could only contrive one which would frighten my reader as I myself had been frightened that night!
>
> Swift as light and as cheering was the idea that broke in upon me. "I have found it! What terrified me will terrify others; and I need only describe the spectre which had haunted my midnight pillow." On the morrow I announced that I had thought of a story. I began that day with the words; It was on a dreary night of November, making only a transcript of the grim terrors of my waking dream.

The far-off volcano made the weather rough on June 16. There was no hope of going on the lake, so they stayed inside. To entertain themselves they read Fantasmagoriana, ou Recueil d' Histoires d' Apparitions, de Spectres, Revenans. They also discussed Samuel Taylor Coleridge's long narrative poem, Christabel. It is spooky and sexual. John Murray had published it on May 25, 1816. As the reading led to a dramatic incident, the poem should be described briefly.

Christabel is the story of two women. Christabel goes into the woods to pray by a large oak tree; she hears a strange noise and finds Geraldine, who tells her she had been abducted by riders. Christabel pities her and takes her home with her. On the way they encounter a number of supernatural signs, like a mysterious flame on a dead fire.

When they get to Christabel's, Geraldine undresses. Her body, she shows Christabel, has some strange mark on it:

> Like one that shuddered, she unbound
> The cincture from beneath her breast:
> Her silken robe, and inner vest,
> Dropt to her feet, and in full view,
> Behold! her bosom and half her side
> A sight to dream of, not to tell!
> And she is to sleep by Christabel.
>
> (246–48)

The unfinished poem ends here.

I have suggested that there was at the very least a homoerotic strain to the relationship between Byron and Polidori. Some modern critics stress lesbian readings of Coleridge's poem.

The effect of the poem on Shelley was violent. Did Shelley sense an erotic charge or a disappointment between Byron and Polidori, one wonders? Polidori wrote:

> Twelve o'clock, really began to talk ghostly. Lord Byron repeated some verses of Coleridge's Christabel, of the witch's breast; when silence ensued, and Shelley, suddenly shrieking and putting his hands to his head, ran out of the room with a candle. Threw water in his face, and after gave him ether. He was looking at Mrs. Shelley, and suddenly thought of a woman he had heard of who had eyes instead of nipples, which horrified him.

Byron later told John Murray that Polidori was basically reporting accurately. Polidori clearly had some ether with him in case Byron needed it.

When Shelley had recovered, Byron suggested; "We will each write a ghost story." That suggestion changed literary history. Everyone agreed. We do not know some details. For example, did they all sit together as they started their stories, or did they all go to their bedrooms? In the prologue to his *The Vampyre*, Polidori pushed the start of his own writing a day later to June 17. The bad weather would last another two days.

Byron's story was only as he said, "A Fragment," and an unfinished fragment at that. Shelley, who seems to have started writing not long after he ran shrieking from the room, based his story on his own early experiences. Shelley scholars have tried to find a manuscript, but without success. Mary Shelley's story eventually became *Frankenstein*, but the version she began to write on June 16 was very different from the version she published later. For weeks, every morning Shelley asked her if she had thought of a story yet, and every morning came the disappointing answer, "No." The finished version reflects the mountains Mary had journeyed through. She wrote some of it at Chamonix in the Alps, when it was again raining so hard they had to stay inside. Byron's mistress Clare Clairmont also wrote a story, but no one has ever found it.

Byron's story "A Fragment" influenced Polidori deeply, and in one letter Polidori called his vampire 'a development' of it. Byron's hero is never given a name and was young and innocent. The villain of Byron's tale, Augustus Darvell, was the very opposite.

"Darvell had already travelled extensively," Byron writes at the start. The nameless hero-narrator hopes to persuade Darvell that they should go East together. Many passages are worth quoting in full. "This wish I first hinted," the narrator says, "and then expressed: his answer, though I had partly expected it, gave me all the pleasure of surprise – he consented; and, after the requisite arrangement, we commenced our voyages."

Quickly Byron lands his two characters in Smyrna in Turkey. Darvell is not happy and suffers "an oppression on his mind," which gets worse as they travel through marshes, passing forlorn huts and some abandoned mosques. Finally, they stop at a cemetery, "the turbaned tombstones of which were the sole indication that human life had ever been a sojourner in this wilderness."

Darvell finds it hard to stand up and asks for water. To the narrator's surprise, Darvell describes the spot where it was to be found, "at a small well for camels, a few hundred yards to the right."

"I said to Darvell, 'How did you know this?'" – as far as the narrator was concerned, this was a desolate spot where no one would want to stay.

When the servant who accompanies them fetches the water, Darvell says melodramatically; "This is the end of my journey, and of my life; I came here to die; but I have a request to make, a command – for such my last words must be. –You will observe it?'"

"Most certainly; but I have better hopes," the narrator replies. Darvell ignores his optimism.

"I have no hopes, nor wishes, but this," Darvell pauses dramatically, "conceal my death from every human being." He then asks his companion to swear "an oath of great solemnity."

After some hesitation, the narrator swears the oath. Darvell then "removed a seal ring from his finger, on which were some Arabic characters, and presented it to me." He went on to say:

> On the ninth day of the month, at noon precisely (what month you please, but this must be the day), you must fling this ring into the salt springs which run into the Bay of Eleusis; the day after, at the same hour, you must repair to the ruins of the temple of Ceres and wait one hour.

"Why," the narrator asks, not unreasonably.
"You will see."
"The ninth day of the month, you say."
"The ninth."
The narrator realizes it is the ninth day of the month. Then something remarkable happens.

> A stork, with a snake in her beak, perched upon a tombstone near us; and, without devouring her prey, appeared to be steadfastly

regarding us. I know not what impelled me to drive it away, but the attempt was useless; she made a few circles in the air and returned exactly to the same spot.

Darvell points to the snake carrying bird, "and smiled – he spoke – I know not whether to himself or to me – but the words were only, 'Tis well!'"

"What is well? What do you mean?"

"No matter; you must bury me here this evening, and exactly where that bird is now perched."

Darvell gives instructions as to how best his death could be concealed and finishes by saying; "You perceive that bird?"

"Certainly."

"And the serpent writhing in her beak?"

The narrator points out; "it is her natural prey. But it is odd that she does not devour it."

Darvell smiles "in a ghastly manner, and whispers; 'It is not yet time!' As he speaks, the stork flies away – presumably with the snake still in its beak.

"My eyes followed it for a moment – it could hardly be longer than ten might be counted. I felt Darvell's weight, as it were, increase upon my shoulder, and, turning to look upon his face, perceived that he was dead!

I was shocked with the sudden certainty which could not be mistaken – his countenance in a few minutes became nearly black. I should have attributed so rapid a change to poison, had I not been aware that he had no opportunity of receiving it unperceived.

They "scooped a shallow grave upon the spot which Darvell had indicated," buried him and laid some withered grass on it.

There had been not been one mention of vampires. Byron ended the story in one sentence. "Between astonishment and grief, I was tearless."

Before seeing how Polidori developed the story and how it inspired his vampire creation, we need to look at the theology he studied as a teenager at Ampleforth with the monks, who were supposed to keep him away from bad influences. The monks were in a tradition of teachers that went back to mediaeval times when theologians pondered the issue of how many angels could stand on a pinhead. In the 1810s demonologists had similar rows about demons, and estimates ranged from a low of under a million to over 4.666666 million.

7

THEOLOGY, CHILD ABUSE AND THE VAMPIRE 'SYNDROME'

This chapter contains graphic material that some readers may find upsetting. Not suitable for younger readers.

Christian demonology is a complex subject, and this chapter merely highlights a few points of vampiric relevance. Unlike vampires, demons are missionaries, as their purpose is to induce humans to sin, mainly in two ways – by testing their faith in God and by tempting all-too-human flesh to indulge in every kind of fornication.

Gregory of Nyssa, in the fourth century, had typical pornographic fantasies for an early father of the Church. He believed male and female demons did the angelic hump with other demons and with women, who were unlikely to resist woefully attractive demons. Gregory's fantasies would not have been out of place in *Playboy*, as he imagined orgies where men and women joined with demons, not to mention the many legions of angels, like cherubim, and of dark infesting powers like incubi and succubi. One is tempted to add sexcubi.

As I said at the start, one challenge of this book was having to cover the silly and the serious. Rouen Cathedral has gargoyles at the front for a good reason. In the ninth century, Romanus, the former chancellor of one of Charlemagne's descendants, Clotaire II, saved the nearby countryside from a monster called *Gargouille*. Charlemagne is a major figure in early mediaeval Europe history. He was crowned as Emperor of the Romans in 800 by the Pope and has been described as the father of Europe. The Holy Roman Empire only collapsed at the end of the 1914 war. Brexiteers would argue it has now been revived in the unholy state of the European Community.

Gargouille is said to have been a typical dragon – bat-like wings, a long neck, scales and breathing fire from its mouth. The dragon seems to have had had many characteristics of a flame-throwing vampire with scales. Miraculously, Romanus subdued the creature with a crucifix. The monster was led back to Rouen and burned, but its head and neck would not crumble to ash. Its head was then mounted on the walls of the newly built church to scare off evil spirits. The head became the first-ever gargoyle.

About 800 years after it had ended its life with so little dignity, the dragon got its revenge on Rouen. Joan of Arc had just saved France. Gilles de Rais, who helped her, appears in George Bernard Shaw's great play as a bluff soldier; he takes the peasant girl to see the Dauphin. Joan outsmarts the nobles and takes command of the French army that drives the English away from Orleans.

Joan's triumph does not last long, because her countrymen give up. She is betrayed to the Inquisition, who accuse her of every known sin, including fornication with demons. She claims to hear the voices of saints, but the Inquisition insist they are the voices of devils. Joan makes matters worse because she does not wear dresses like a peasant girl should but armour like a soldier. She is accused of being a pervert, a heretic who has had intercourse with demons.

Joan of Arc was burnt at the stake in 1429. Shaw ended his play with her plea, "How long O Lord?" before his saints were recognized. It took five centuries before she was beatified.

Shaw did not mention, however, what happened rather more immediately to Gilles de Rais. Five years after Joan was burned, he was accused of having tortured and murdered more than 500 children. He was literally a Satanic abuser. Forty-seven charges were brought against him, including 'the conjuration of demons' and sexual perversions against children.

In his 1971 biography, Jean Benedetti tells how the children who fell into Rais' hands were treated:

> [The boy] was pampered and dressed in better clothes than he had ever known. The evening began with a large meal and heavy drinking, which acted as a stimulant. The boy was then taken to an upper room to which only Gilles and his immediate circle were admitted. There he was confronted with the true nature of his situation. The shock thus produced on the boy was an initial source of pleasure for Gilles.

At the trial, the prosecution said;

> to practise his debauches with the said boys and girls, against the dictation of nature, he first took his rod in his hand and rubbed it so it became erect and sticking out; then placing it between the limbs of the boys or girls, not bothering with the natural female receptacle, and rubbed his rod or virile member on the belly of the said boys and girls with much libidinous excitement until he emitted his sperm on their stomachs.

Gilles' body servant testified to the truth of that and added when he took the victim down, de Rais comforted the child and assured him he only wanted to play with him. Before killing him.

Perhaps de Rais most obvious vampiric trait was that.

> Sometimes he made an incision behind the neck to make them die slowly, at which he became very excited, and while they were bleeding to death he would sometimes masturbate on them, and sometimes he would do this after they had died, and their bodies were still warm.

This is one of the most obviously sexual links to vampirism and the 'vampire syndrome', which is discussed later.

De Rais testified that

> when the said children were dead, he kissed them and those who
> had the most handsome limbs and heads he held up to admire
> them, and had their bodies cruelly cut open and took delight at
> the sight of their inner organs; and very often when the children
> were dying he sat on their stomachs and took pleasure in seeing
> them die and laughed.

De Rais case is especially interesting because of the links mentioned earlier between vampires and child abuse. The literature here
needs some unravelling. Butz (1993) has argued in Jungian terms
that for victims, the vampire represents the negative aspect of the
healer archetype.

Perhaps this is addressed more usefully in a paper called *Vampire or
Pinocchio*. Michel St Yves and Bruno Pellerin surveyed offenders in Que-
bec's Regional Reception Centre. They first asked if their subjects had
been molested as a child? "This is the unavoidable question faced by
all offenders who are accused or convicted of a sex crime." They came
up with a vague answer that from 30% to 60% of them – with pae-
dophiles predominant – said they had been molested. The figure of
30% agrees with research by the National Children's Home, which I
reported for Channel 4's Dispatches in a television programme called
The Last Taboo.

The National Children's Home claimed that one-third of child
abusers had been abused as children. Two-thirds obviously did not
inflict on others what had been inflicted on them. Trying to explain
why they did not has remained elusive.

St Yves and Pellerin said:

> This perception of "cause and effect" is supported by various
> writers who believe that the presence of unresolved sexual
> trauma. Some even emphasize that sex crimes are often a repro-
> duction of previously experienced sexual abuse. They call this the
> "vampire" syndrome.

They suspected some sex offenders were exaggerating as a way of explaining or excusing their own sex crimes. No one knows how common this is, but an American study of sex offenders showed that, after they were told that they would be subject to a polygraph test, the percentage of those claiming sexual victimization dropped from 67% to 29%.

St Yves and Pellerin also studied whether signs of early victimization could be found in the criminal behaviour of sex offenders; 85.7% of the subjects reported having been abused by a man. Subjects who claimed to have been abused while under 12 years of age were more likely to have abused a similarly prepubescent child, but only 57.1% of those who claimed to have been abused molested prepubescent children.

In *The Last Taboo*, one of the men I interviewed claimed that his father would take baths with him and abuse him from when he was 3 years old. That made him an abuser. His father then farmed him out to some of his friends.

St Yves and Bellerin found that 36.5% of rapists also reported that they had been abused before the age of 12. This shows that the age of sexual victimization is not a good predictor of paedophilia. Subjects who reported sexual victimization also reported victimization in several other areas of their lives. More of them had been exposed to violence, substance abuse and exhibited behavioural problems before the age of 18 and committed sex offences (as juveniles and as adults). The results of these studies made them question whether abusers had actually often been abused. Studies that make that claim are usually based on self-reporting. It is therefore possible that some subjects invent sexual victimization scenarios (which St Yves and Bellerin call the Pinocchio syndrome) or that they magnify in order to excuse or justify their crimes. The vampire syndrome does not explain the high percentage (about 50%) of individuals who reported that they had not been molested in childhood but who still committed sex crimes. Conversely, many children who were abused never became abusers.

It is time to note a few lighter details, remembering that gargoyles also look comic. In October 2009, *Playboy* carried vampires on its front cover. Bloodlust was the main story of that edition. Many readers thought the sexiest piece and pic was "Love Bites." Another article was called "Bad to the Bone." All very vampiric.

In his many vituperative pamphlets that sparked the sixteenth-century Reformation, Martin Luther accused the Catholic Church itself of vampiric tendencies because in the Mass, the blood of Christ was drunk literally. Luther made this into a symbolic act. In likening the Catholic Mass to a vampire blood fest, he ignored the fact that the blood was not the result of any biting. Luther never let facts get in the way of polemics and depicted the Pope as the anti-Christ. Catholics continue to discuss vampirism, however.

A recent novel, *Jennifer the Damned*, testifies to the continuing Catholic interest. A 16-year-old orphan vampire is adopted by an order of nuns and matures into her immortal, blood-sucking glory. Then all hell literally breaks loose. Yet with every taste of blood, Jennifer Carshaw longs for something even more exquisite: the capacity to experience true love. As she struggles to balance her murderous secret life with homework, cross-country practice and her first boyfriend, Jennifer delves into the terrifying questions surrounding her undead existence. She is driven by the unexpectedly human need to understand why she is doomed to a life she never chose.

Jennifer the Damned re-examines the vampire as a conflicted and complex being. She is the quintessential vampire but also a sympathetic young woman full of spiritual anxieties, gifted, ironic and hopeful. Unlike most vampires – perhaps this is due to the nuns – she yearns for love as well as blood.

It is now time to time travel back to the Villa Diodati.

8

THE FIRST STORY

According to Polidori, Byron intended to have Darvell reappear as a vampire. There has been much scholarly debate on whether Byron meant to write more – why after all did he call his fragment *The Vampyre*? He dashed it off perhaps because the ghost stories were a game to pass the time and because he meant all those in the villa to produce something quickly. The reality would be very different. Both *Frankenstein* and Polidori's vampire would need months of hard work.

Polidori did not start on June 16, as he went dancing, but yet again his body betrayed him, and he "felt such horrid pain [I] was forced to stop." His sprained ankle was playing up again. "The ghost stories are begun by all but me," he wrote. It was only the next day after bemoaning, "My leg much worse," that Polidori added: "Began my ghost story after tea." Tea seems rather tame when he was conjuring up a blood feast.

Polidori's vampire story should always be seen in the context of his difficult relationship with his father. He owed his life – and so his blood – to his father, but his father was, he felt sometimes, sucking him dry.

The links between Polidori's story and Byron's also need to be looked at carefully. Polidori himself was a good writer, so again, I quote some of the text in detail.

Polidori's story starts darkly in the middle of winter when a noble-man appears in London high society. The man could "throw fear into those breasts where thoughtlessness reigned." Just looking at some-one's face allowed him to pierce "through to the inward workings of the heart. His peculiarities caused him to be invited to every house; all wished to see him." Women found the stranger very attractive. Lady Mercer, who did not take her marriage seriously, "threw herself in his way." Critics argue that Lady Mercer was based on one of Byron's lovers, Lady Caroline Lamb, who would have made a perfect patient for any psychoanalyst.

At about the same time, Polidori wrote, a rich young gentle-man came to London. Aubrey was romantic and naïve. He added that Aubrey "had, hence, that high romantic feeling of honour and candour, which daily ruins so many milliners' apprentices." Vice was clearly an occupational hazard for them. Aubrey imagined that the dreams of poets were the realities of life. Mothers wanted the nice, and rich, young man for their daughters. Any hopes of a happy life were dashed when he met the nobleman described earlier, who was Lord Ruthven. Aubrey became fascinated by him. The name of Ruth-ven is telling. Byron's mother was pursued by Lord Grey De Ruthyn, and Byron may also have been molested by him.

Aubrey learned Ruthven was about to leave England. He offered to travel with him and was delighted when Ruthven agreed. Unlike Byron, Polidori gave many details of their journey across Europe, which allowed Aubrey to study Lord Ruthven at close quarters. He was generous but paradoxical, "in his liberality; – the idle, the vaga-bond, and the beggar, received from his hand more than enough to relieve their immediate wants." But Ruthven did not give to the so-called deserving poor, who were sent away not just empty-handed but "with a hardly suppressed sneer." If helping a man or woman would allow him or her "to wallow in his lust, or to sink him still deeper in his iniquity, he was sent away with rich charity." The charity was cursed. In the worst cases, those Ruthven 'helped' were led to the scaffold; in the best to "the lowest and the most abject misery."

As they went through Europe, Aubrey was surprised at the way Ruthven "sought for the centres of all fashionable vice." These were mainly casinos, it seems. Ruthven gambled and usually won, but whether he won or lost, "it was always with the same unchanging face, with which he generally watched the society around:"

When Ruthven met a likely victim, "his eyes sparkled with more fire than that of the cat whilst dallying with the half-dead mouse." Having suggested early that Ruthven was evil, Polidori now called Ruthven 'a fiend' who lured good people to their destruction.

When they got to Rome, Aubrey got letters from his guardians, which "astonished him (and) seemed to give him sufficient reason for the belief" that Ruthven was the personification of evil. Aubrey should leave him, as Ruthven's character "was dreadfully vicious, for that the possession of irresistible powers of seduction, rendered his licentious habits more dangerous to society." Sex and the vampire were always close.

Ruthven had made some outrageous demands of one woman he had seduced in London. Before getting entangled with him, she was "the pinnacle of unsullied virtue," but Ruthven mired her "down to the lowest abyss of infamy and degradation."

The same seemed likely to happen in Rome. Aubrey realized that "his Lordship was endeavouring to work upon the inexperience of the daughter of the lady whose house he chiefly frequented." The two had arranged to meet, "which would most likely end in the ruin of an innocent, though thoughtless girl." Aubrey asked Ruthven "his intentions with respect to the lady." Ruthven just laughed in his face.

It is not possible to know how quickly Polidori was writing, but he seems to have been under some stress again. He often quarrelled with Byron and Shelley in June, July and August. He had "a long explanation with Shelley and Lord Byron about my conduct." There was an extreme example when Polidori "threatened to shoot Shelley one day on the water." This, according to Dowden, was due to "some hare-brained quarrel with Shelley leading to a challenge for a duel." Horses were twice the cause. Polidori was accused of laming one. In view of all this, it seems rather staid to say, as Polidori did, that his conduct towards Byron "was considered not to be correct." On August 29, Shelley and the two women left Geneva to return to England.

In Polidori's vampire story, Aubrey left Rome, not for England, but for Athens. There, he fell in love with a dazzling Greek girl, Ianthe, who seemed like a gazelle when she danced though "one would have thought the gazelle a poor type of her beauties." She went with Aubrey to see many antiquities. He was entranced.

Ianthe was also a good storyteller, and here Polidori's story goes way beyond Byron, for he does introduce vampires, as we know them now. Ianthe knew of one "who had passed years amidst his friends, and dearest ties, forced every year, by feeding upon the life of a lovely female to prolong his existence for the ensuing months." Aubrey tries to humour Ianthe out of her absurd belief, but he fails. Ianthe's family know some old men who have a vampire living amongst them, and "several of their near relatives and children had been found marked with the stamp of the fiend's appetite." Aubrey is especially horrified because it was "a pretty accurate description of Lord Ruthven." Ianthe's parents were "pale with horror" at any talk of vampires.

In horror tales, however, the heroes often can't control their curiosity. Ianthe's parents try to dissuade him from visiting a wood where no Greek would ever tread. Vampires meet there for orgies. Aubrey is an English gentleman, however, and "a superior, infernal power, the very name of which apparently made their blood freeze" is not going to deter him. The battle of Waterloo had been won on the playing fields of Eton, after all. Vampires would pale before English sangfroid.

The next morning as Aubrey sets off alone. Ianthe begs him to return before nightfall. (Polidori was the first writer to make a central point of the fact that vampires could not stand sunlight.) Aubrey did promise Ianthe, but he could not keep his promise. Night fell fast while he was on the road. A storm swirled wild. His horse panics and gallops away – straight towards a hovel.

As he gets near the hovel, Aubrey hears a woman shriek, and then mocking laughter. He forces the door open and finds himself in pitch black. But some creature lurks in the dark; it lurks, laughs and snarls for good measure: "Again baffled!" The creature "whose strength seemed superhuman" grabs Aubrey, who is "hurled with enormous force against the ground."

The vampire moves in for the kill, but before he can taste blood, a group of spoilsport men holding blazing torches turn up. Any light, not just the sun, would foil the monster. Aubrey asks his rescuers to search for the woman he had heard shrieking. He would soon wish he hadn't. By torchlight he sees her "airy form." But it is the lifeless body of Ianthe. The vampire had been satisfied, as "upon her neck and breast was blood, and upon her throat were the marks of teeth having opened the vein." The men who had saved Aubrey pointed, crying, simultaneously struck with horror, "A Vampyre! a Vampyre!"

It was a dramatic debut for the monster.

They bring Ianthe's body back to Athens. Her distressed parents "looked at Aubrey and pointed to the corpse. They were inconsolable; both died broken-hearted." Aubrey is seized with "a most violent fever and was often delirious."

Ruthven himself now reaches Athens and, for once, he has muzzled sneering. Remarkably he does his best to console Aubrey. When he recovers from his delirium, Aubrey is horrified "at the sight of him whose image he had now combined with that of a Vampyre."

Aubrey can find no peace in Athens because he keeps on thinking of Ianthe. Polidori then introduced a surprising twist, which shows he could be a good storyteller. Though Ruthven is still sneering, Aubrey suggests they visit parts of Greece neither of them had yet seen. They are ambushed in a river valley. They "were startled by the whistling of bullets close to their heads, and by the echoed report of several guns." Ruthven is hit in the shoulder; the robbers surround them.

Robbers are easier to pacify than vampires. In his text Polidori does not explain why he then agreed to pay the robbers a fine ransom if they carry his wounded companion to a nearby cabin. Given his feelings about Lord Ruthven, the gesture is extraordinary; he agrees to get the ransom money to save Ruthven. When he returns after two days, he is shocked by what he sees.

> Lord Ruthven's strength rapidly decreased; in two days mortification ensued, and death seemed advancing with hasty steps . . . but towards the close of the last evening, his mind became apparently uneasy, and his eye often fixed upon Aubrey.

"Assist me!" Ruthven begs. "You may save me – you may do more than that – I mean not my life, I heed the death of my existence as little as that of the passing day; but you may save my honour, your friend's honour."

"How? tell me how? I would do anything," Aubrey replies. Again Polidori offers no explanation of why he is so willing to help a man he thinks is evil. It could be suggested that being a vampire Ruthven was able to impose his will, but the text does not say.

> "I need but little – my life ebbs apace – I cannot explain the whole – but if you would conceal all you know of me, my honour were free from stain in the world's mouth – and if my death were unknown for some time in England – I – I – but life."

"It shall not be known," Aubrey promises.

> "Swear by all your soul reveres, by all your nature fears, swear that, for a year and a day you will not impart your knowledge of my crimes or death to any living being in any way, whatever may happen, or whatever you may see."

Ruthven's eyes seem to burst from their sockets.

"I swear!" says Aubrey.

Then Ruthven "sunk laughing upon his pillow and breathed no more."

Byron ended his story with Darvell's death. For Polidori, the death of Ruthven was a prelude to the climax. Aubrey goes to rest but has "the presentiment of something horrible awaiting him."

Aubrey decides to return to England. As he waits for a boat to take him to Italy, he searches Ruthven's suitcases. He finds "a case containing several weapons of offence, more or less adapted to ensure the death of the victim. There were several daggers and ataghans." Aubrey finds a sheath decorated in the same style as the dagger that killed Ianthe, and then the weapon itself; "his horror may be imagined when he discovered that it fitted, though peculiarly shaped, the sheath he held in his hand."

On his way home, Aubrey stops in Rome and tries to find the young woman he had stopped from meeting Ruthven. She has not been heard of since Ruthven left the city. Aubrey fears that Lord Ruthven had killed her too.

Byron left Darvell in the East; in Polidori's, story the climax was in London. His sister is overjoyed to see him. They go to a party. While Aubrey is standing alone in a corner, he remembers that the first time he had seen Lord Ruthven was in that very place. "Aubrey felt himself suddenly seized by the arm, and a voice he recognized too well, sounded in his ear; 'Remember your oath', it snarls."

Aubrey does not have the courage to turn around, "fearful of seeing a spectre that would blast him, when he perceived, at a little distance, the same figure which had attracted his notice on this spot upon his first entry into society." He escapes and drives home.

He paces his room.

> Lord Ruthven again before him − circumstances started up in dreadful array − the dagger − his oath. He roused himself, he could not believe it possible − the dead rise again! − He thought his imagination had conjured up the image his mind was resting upon. It was impossible that it could be real.

He goes back to the soiree and sees "his sister surrounded by several people when a man turned round. It was Ruthven who whispered urgently; 'Remember your oath!' − He did not dare to turn, but, hurrying his sister, soon reached home." Again.

Aubrey is bewildered, hardly surprising since he had seen Ruthven die, and scared. He had sworn the oath. He thinks of killing Ruthven, but the man seems unable to give up the ghost, as it were.

Aubrey feels he has to warn his friends they have a 'fiend' amongst them, but he behaves so strangely, his sister begs him to recover himself. His guardians, fearing he is going mad, get a physician to live in the house and take constant care of him. Aubrey is so incoherent he has to be kept in his room. Only his sister can communicate with him and "then he would sometimes start, and, seizing her hands, with looks that severely afflicted her, he would desire her not to touch him." He pleaded; "Oh, do not touch him – if your love for me is aught, do not go near him!"

When she asks who Aubrey meant, his only answer is, "'True! true!' and again he sank into a state, whence not even she could rouse him." After many months he begins to rally and, even from time to time, "he would count upon his fingers a definite number, and then smile."

Then on December 31, one of his guardians and his doctor tell him it is how sad he is in such a desperate state when his sister is going to be married the next day. Aubrey asks anxiously who the groom is. The Earl of Marsden, they tell him. Aubrey congratulates his sister and kisses her; she is pleased her brother can be affectionate again. Then he sees she is wearing a locket, and "opening it, what was his surprise at beholding the features of the monster, who had so long influenced his life. He seized the portrait in a paroxysm of rage and trampled it under foot." Then he pleads with her to "swear that she would never wed this monster."

Then Aubrey hears Ruthven's voice warning him not to forget his oath. His guardians tell his sister to leave him. He collapses before them and implores them to delay the wedding – if only for one day. He's mad as a hatter, they think, and, utterly baffled, leave.

When Ruthven hears of Aubrey's acute distress, he can "hardly hide his pleasure" at the fact that everyone thinks Aubrey has lost his mind. Cunningly and with his tongue waxed silver, Ruthven persuades his bride to be to ignore what her brother had said. Ruthven knows "so well how to use the serpent's art, or such was the will of fate, that he gained her affections." The marriage will go ahead the following day.

Aubrey bribes the servants to take his sister a letter. He implores her to wait before marrying, but the servants betray him, as they also think he is mad, and hand the letter to the doctor, who takes it as more proof Aubrey is insane. The letter never reaches Aubrey's sister.

The morning of the wedding, Aubrey escapes and rushes to the wedding. Ruthven grabs hold of him and whispers; "Remember your oath, and know, if not my bride today, your sister is dishonoured. Women are frail!"

Aubrey has yet another seizure and has to be taken home to bed. No one tells his sister because no one wants to spoil her wedding day. She is married and goes off, seemingly normal, on her honeymoon with her husband. Aubrey becomes weaker and, "the effusion of blood produced symptoms of the near approach of death. He desired his sister's guardians might be called, and when the midnight hour had struck, he related composedly what the reader has perused – he died immediately after."

It was all too late. "The guardians hastened to protect Miss Aubrey; but when they arrived, it was too late. Lord Ruthven had disappeared."

Polidori's last line was finely melodramatic; "Aubrey's sister had glutted the thirst of a VAMPYRE!"

THE PRIME VAMPIRE STORY

For many reasons, Polidori's story is rightly considered the first vampire story. First, he makes it clear, as Byron did not, that the villain was a vampire. Second, Ruthven needs blood as much as oxygen. Third, he cannot stand the light. Fourth, he never seems to die. Some essential features of later vampire stories are still missing, as there is no hint that one could kill a vampire by driving a stake through his heartless heart – a lurid detail that came from Scottish lore of vampire fairies – and also no hint that the best way to protect oneself is to flourish a crucifix at the creature.

I mentioned the heredity of Prince Charles, who includes Vlad the Impaler among his ancestors. Glamis Castle, where Charles' grandmother, the late Queen Mother, grew up, has skull and blood traditions. One story claims that in each generation of the family a vampire is born and hidden in a secret room. The servants at Glamis were not innocent either. A serving woman was said to have been caught leaning over a body and drinking the victim's blood. She was walled up alive in the castle. The legends may have some basis in fact. Somewhere in the 16-foot-thick (4.9m) walls is the famous room of skulls, where the misguided Ogilvie family were bricked up. In 1486 they sought protection from their enemies at Glamis; their hosts betrayed tradition of hospitality, walled them up and let them die of starvation.

Travellers in Scotland were also warned not to fall asleep in a fairy circle, especially after sunset, if they wanted to live. The Baobhan Sith – or vampire fairies – were especially brutal, devoured their victims and ripped out their hearts.

We do not know when Polidori finished his vampire story, though it is plausible that he had finished it by September 5. In his biography of Shelley, Dowden suggested Byron claimed that Polidori 'appropriated' some of Byron's tale. There is nothing in Mary's diary to suggest that, however.

By the end of August, Byron was finally exasperated with his physician. Polidori had even managed to be robbed on the lake, as someone stole the sails of their little boat. The thieves tried to steal the anchors too. Polidori was grounded like a naughty school boy. Less than four months after they had sailed from Dover, Byron decided to give him his 'congé' – the French word for dismissal.

A few days later, for once, Polidori earned his salary as a doctor. An apothecary sold Byron some magnesia which aroused Polidori's suspicions. He insisted it on testing it, which was just as well as; "Found it bad by experiment of sulphuric acid colouring it red rose-colour." Byron was not so impressed, even though Polidori was.

Any hope that Byron might change his mind and keep Polidori on was dashed, because Polidori now broke his spectacles. Extremely annoyed, Byron now decided to subject Polidori to an ordeal. He ordered him to give an account of the incident in front of two physicians. There was then a kind of mock trial "before five judges; had an advocate to plead. I pleaded for myself; laughed at the advocate. Lost his cause on the plea of calumny; made me pay 12 florins for the broken spectacles and costs."

Fact was a dramatic as fiction. When there was no reprieve, Polidori ran to his room. He had decided to poison himself and was wondering whether to leave a suicide note when Byron came in and tried to calm him down. The poet alternated, as he had often done, between being harsh and kind. Polidori was so grateful he burst into tears. But any reconciliation was very temporary.

On September 15, Hobhouse wrote in his diary that he helped Polidori settle his 'involved accounts' with Byron. Polidori, Hobhouse continued,

> does not answer to Madame de Stael's account of a happy man. . . . Took leave of him, poor fellow. He is anything but an amiable man, and has a most unmeasurable ambition as well as inordinate vanity; the true ingredients of misery.

Polidori left Switzerland on September 15. It took him five days to work up the courage to write to his father to admit that Byron had dismissed him. Polidori tried to be mature; "We have parted, our tempers did not agree." He added guiltily – but then he was often guilty to his father – "I believe the fault if any has been on my part I am not accustomed to having a master and therefore my conduct was not free and easy." In his diary, he said that Byron "determined upon our parting – not upon any quarrel, but on account of our not suiting."

Byron gave him £70 – £50 for three months and £20 for the trip. Polidori had debts to pay which took care of much of this money.

From now on he was always short of money, a problem vampires rarely had.

Polidori struggled to reach Italy, and then he had to leave Milan on October 30 after a row in a theatre which took place when Byron was present:

> I got into the coach with only 5 louis in my pocket, leaving my books in the care of di Breme, and left Milan with rage and grief so struggling in my breast that tears often started in my eyes, and all I could think of was revenge.

It shows the extent to which he was disturbed that Polidori did not just lose his dog but did not even notice the fact he had lost the animal.

Leaving Byron would not mean the end of Polidori's 'scrapes'.

9

SUCKING OUT ENERGY – AND THE PASSIVE-AGGRESSIVE PERSONALITY

I suggested earlier that both Byron and Polidori had some character-istics of the psychic vampire. Though I have been critical of academic studies of vampirism, here the Atlanta Vampire Alliance has made one very useful contribution.

Dion Fortune wrote of psychic parasitism in relation to vampir-ism as early as 1930 in her book, *Psychic Self-Defense*. One wonders whether J.K. Rowling read her in creating the job of professor of Defence against the Dark Arts at Hogwarts. Fortune considered psy-chic vampirism to be a combination of psychological problems and psychic disturbance. The vampire is also a disturbed spirit. The label 'psychic vampire' was popularized in the 1960s by Anton LaVey and his Church of Satan. He used the term to mean a spiritually or emo-tionally weak person who drains vital energy from others. There has been an occult revival in the Soviet Union, and the terms 'energy vampire' and 'psychic vampire' have become popular there.

The psychic vampire featured in the TV show, *Dirk Gently's Holistic Detective Agency*, where the characters known as the Rowdy Three are called 'Psychic Vampires' because they feed on psychic energy. It has been my fate to know at least four people who often drained me of energy. They were not vampires, but for a variety of reasons, they demanded so much that I left any encounter with them exhausted. The first was my mother. In my book *Home Alone*, I described how she became increasingly demanding as she got older. She was an intelligent and attractive woman, but my father left her, leaving her bereft. She began to lose her eyesight and became depressed.

One of my mother's requests was that I persuade a psychiatrist friend of mine to give her a prescription so that she could kill herself. If I were a dutiful son, I would give her the drug and sit with her as she died. She had been trained as a lawyer and knew it would have been illegal for my friend or I to assist in her suicide. In the end, she hoarded many sleeping pills that her doctor had prescribed for her and killed herself. It was a tragic end and upset her two grandsons as well as me. I was left wondering if I had been unkind and failed her. She was still physically quite well. I found it hard to recognize she had enough of life because of her constant demands.

The other relative I shall call Mrs Driver. She was the daughter of a respectable family, but from the age of 13, she felt her parents favoured her brother and sister. When she was in her late twenties, her sister and her brother both suffered tragedies. As a result, their parents gave them money. Mrs Driver could never forget that and kept on calculating the profit she could have made if she had been given money too. It was an obsession to which she returned time and again.

Her husband left her, and her relationship with her children broke down. In the end she lost much money in a dubious transaction – and that too became an endlessly repeated topic. She had been pilloried unjustly.

The other two were professional encounters. The first was a woman who ran a seaside repertory company which I joined at the age of 16 when I was determined to be an actor. Mary L claimed to have been a mistress of the Prince of Wales. She talked constantly about her experiences, and she certainly knew some stars. She arranged for me to meet Richard Harris, who played Dumbledore in the first Harry Potter films. She ran our theatre company ruthlessly, smoked constantly and never listened. Once when we had an audience of only two she insisted we still perform an abominable play in which I played a Welsh village idiot with a dreadful Welsh accent.

My fourth energy sucker was the most dramatic. Lola was a would-be writer and married to a film producer. To escape from her, he hired me to put on a play she claimed to have written. During rehearsals, he fled to Spain. Typically, the play was unfinished. Her husband hired a writer to actually write it. Lola's background was, as she said herself, utterly remarkable. She claimed to have been born under a sacred tree in central America. This gave her unique insights, so Lola objected to most of the writer's ideas. The play began as a comedy, but in the last act, it was revealed that her son was the Messiah. Which made her the Virgin Mary.

Unhappy with the play, she got together with some friends and invaded the stage on the first night to denounce the whole enterprise. The audience were not sure if this was meant to be part of the play. When some critics said it was a clever idea, Lola said that if only I had listened to her, the play would have been a huge success.

Freud did offer an account of how children turned into sadists, but no one has explained the causes of passive-aggressive behaviour properly. Its roots are said to be complex and deep-seated but remain vague. The New York University Medical Centre defines a passive-aggressive individual as someone who "may appear to comply or act appropriately, but actually behaves negatively and passively resists." This description echoes the four people I have described. Passive-aggressive individuals are unreasonable to deal with, uncomfortable to be around, rarely express their hostility directly and usually cannot stop doing it.

A catalogue of conditions that are associated with passive aggression have been suggested. They include attention deficit hyperactivity disorder, stress, anxiety disorders, depression, conduct disorder, the splendidly named oppositional defiant disorder (which means patients don't do what their teachers, psychiatrists or other who have authority over them want them to do), bipolar disorder and schizotypal personality disorder. They also abuse alcohol and cocaine. Somehow heroin and glue sniffing were left out. The

NYU list hardly excludes any psychiatric problem and is perhaps not very useful.

The lack of a theory which could be tested has not stopped some psychologists giving advice on how to deal with the passive-aggressive personality. It is banal, usually. My own experience suggests such individuals do suck out energy and are impossible to handle. Run away if possible. The psychic vampire has stamina – a quality which Polidori needed.

10

IN PRINT

Polidori's uncle, Luigi, was known in Arezzo for his skill in curing typhoid fever. Luigi had received a letter from his brother in which Gaetano told him he was worried about Polidori. Luigi realized why the moment Polidori got to his house. His nephew was so tired he just grabbed some food and went to sleep. The next day Polidori wrote to reassure his father that he was well and that he had been welcomed very warmly. He stayed a few days, most of which were spent studying the *Osteologia*, a treatise on bones which Polidori's grandfather had ambitiously written in rhyme. Gaetano translated and published it in English many years later.

On November 21, Polidori set off back north to Florence. He had only half a scudo, as he had refused to accept help from Luigi because he did not want his uncle to know "how it stood." If his uncle knew, he feared his father would be told, as they wrote to each other. Polidori would have dreaded his father's disapproval. Gaetano was excellent at guilt.

In Florence, Polidori "as a last chance looked at the Post Office." There he found two letters from his friend, Lloyd. Lloyd was Welsh and his real name was Ap Griffiths; Polidori had met him in Geneva and saw him again in Milan. The first letter was not helpful, as Lloyd had lost his own purse and so could not help. The second letter was

more cheering. Lloyd had returned to Florence himself now and welcomed Polidori "with great kindness and assured me that while he
had money I should never want."

Lloyd also suggested Polidori settle in Florence as a doctor offering his services to the English residents, who tended to distrust the
locals. Polidori did not accept Lloyd's advice. After just six days in the
city, Polidori set off by boat for Pisa. He was so broke he had to walk
some of the way. When he got to Pisa, he rushed to the post office,
but there were "no letters. In Despair." The phrase summed up his
feelings. The promising physician who, six months earlier, had been
travelling in a grand coach modelled on Napoleon's now could not
afford to hire a mule. He had lost his position, toyed with poisoning
himself, bought books he could not afford and was too proud and
frightened to borrow from his uncle. As a result of these accidents and
self-inflicted disasters, Polidori could not face going back to England
and explaining himself to his father.

Byron himself gives some clue as to how penniless Polidori managed to stay three more months in Italy. He told Murray that he
thought he had managed to find three English patients in Pisa. Their
fees allowed him to stay. Polidori was always restless, though, and
soon left for Ravenna, Bologna and, finally, to Venice, where he met
Byron again. It was a tense encounter.

The poet complained to Murray: "I never was much more disgusted
with any human production than with the eternal nonsense and tracasseries and emptiness and ill-humour and vanity of that young person"
('Tracasseries' is French for annoyances). In Italy, there followed a strange
event which seems to suggest more intimacy than one might expect.
Byron was sometimes unpleasant about his lovers, as he was about
Claire Claremont. Despite all his complaints, Byron trusted Polidori
enough to give him two paintings to bring back to his sister in
England. At the end of his letter to Murray, Byron was kinder, saying
"but he has some talent, and is a man of honour, and has dispositions
of amendment in which he has been aided by a little subsequent experience, and may turn out well." These ambivalences suggest guilt and
that Polidori may have been more than a physician to Byron.

Polidori did not dare ask his father for money to pay for his fare back to England. In his diary, he gives no details about how he managed to travel. It seems likely that the man who was so angry with the physician he had sacked a few months earlier now gave him the money he needed.

As he made for London, Polidori was also carrying a manuscript that would make his name – The Vampyre. It was published in April 1819 in the New Monthly Magazine, but some mystery surrounds how that happened. In the introduction to Ernestus Berchtold, Polidori said that he left one manuscript "in the hands of a lady." Then, somehow, Polidori said the story "appears to have fallen into the hands of some person who sent it to the editor in such a way so to leave so doubtful from his words that I had some difficulty in vindicating it to myself."

Being less than scrupulous, that editor, Henry Colburn decided to publicize it as a new work by Lord Byron, for obvious commercial reasons. Polidori got absolutely no credit. Understandably he was furious, and Byron was too. Both men became even more angry when the story was well received.

As soon as the story came out, Polidori protested to Colburn; "The tale of The Vampyre . . . is not Lord Byron's but was written entirely by me." He demanded "either that a compensation be made me or that its separate publication be instantly suppressed" ("Letter to Colburn" 15–16). In another letter, however, Polidori added that "the groundwork is certainly Lord Byron's, [but] its development is mine."

Byron himself energetically denied he wrote The Vampyre, stating that he "never heard of the work in question until now." That seems a little farfetched given the many meetings he had with Polidori in Italy.

Sales were too good, however, for Colburn to set the record straight quickly. A work by Byron with autobiographical overtones would sell more copies than a tale by an unknown physician. When Colburn was threatened with a lawsuit, he didn't flinch but blamed the fraud on Polidori. Colburn would probably have got away with passing the work off as Byron's if the poet had not insisted the story had nothing to do with him.

Ultimately, Colburn met Polidori. The most the real writer could get out of him was £30. Colburn still was devious about the credit; he did not withdraw the first printing, and Polidori's name only appeared in the second edition. The other three editions that appeared in 1819 and 1820 either had Byron's name as the author or no name at all on the title page.

The story was quickly printed five times. There were complimentary reviews in periodicals like *Blackwoods* and *The Edinburgh Review*. In Europe it became a critical success. The great German writer Goethe, who had no reason to doubt Byron had written it, even called it Byron's masterpiece. Byron was not delighted with that, either.

To clear up the confusion Colburn found so profitable and perhaps because he had been close to Polidori, Byron finally published his own 'Fragment of a Novel'. In the midst of this publishing row, Byron was as usual in difficulties with women – and a letter he wrote to Murray matters in terms of *Vampyre* history. Byron denied that he wrote *The Vampyre* and partially confirmed Polidori's claim that Shelley freaked out one night. What Byron did not confirm was the sexual detail that Shelley hallucinated that the women had eyes on their breasts.

The dramas at Diodati had many consequences for Polidori and the others. Mary Shelley finished *Frankenstein, or the Modern Prometheus* and published a small first edition of 500 copies in January of 1818. The publishers gave her six presentation copies to give away; she put one aside to give to Byron, the man who had started it all.

Mary signed it without giving her name, merely writing "To Lord Byron from the author"; she initially wanted authorial anonymity. She did not fool Byron who wrote to John Murray in May 1819: "Mary Godwin (now Mrs. Shelley) wrote 'Frankenstein' – which you have reviewed thinking it Shelley's – methinks it is a wonderful work for a Girl of nineteen – not nineteen indeed – at that time."

Polidori was eventually acknowledged as the real author of *The Vampyre*, but the book does not seem to have earned him more than the £30 Colburn paid. The publication did at least bring some fame and made it possible for him to publish some of his other works, including *Ernestus Berchtold*, which was subtitled *A Modern Oedipus*. It dealt with an issue that was psychologically acute for him – the hostility of a son to a father. *Ernestus Berchtold* was an ambitious novel, though melodramatic. It confronted more directly the relationship between a son and a father figure, difficult ground for Polidori, as well as the then-fashionable theme of incest. The book was a modest critical success but not enough of one to bring Polidori the work he wanted, writing for London's many periodicals. It only sold 199 copies.

The Vampyre was much more popular than Oedipus revived. Polidori would find that hard to take.

11

VAMPIRES IN THE WARD

Dr Polidori would have been disappointed, perhaps, in the little attention his medical colleagues gave to any pathology vampires might suffer from. The most interesting contribution perhaps has come not from a haematologist but from two chemists, Lionel Milgrom, who perhaps appropriately teaches at Byron's old school, Eton, and David Dolphin. Milgrom, who studied at Liverpool University, headed a research group at Imperial College which explored the potential uses of what one might call 'vampire biochemistry' in the treatment of cancer.

In the 1980s Dolphin suggested that vampires might be suffering from a real disease. He seized on one which has been debated since Alan Bennett's brilliant play *The Madness of George III* and argued that vampires might be suffering from porphyria. In the play, the palace doctors are struck by the fact that the royal urine is an unnatural blue.

Never having heard of porphyria, they see it as a sign of madness.

Porphyria is a constellation of diseases that affect the ability to synthesize an iron-containing molecule called haem. Iron is essential to the body, Lionel Milgrom told me when I met him at the Royal Society of Arts. The biochemistry is complex. Without iron, porphyrin is useless to the body and, put simply, haem carries oxygen in the blood.

The problem comes if this transport system does not work, as Milgrom explained to me, and his 1997 book *The Colours of Life* details the history of porphyrins, how they work and what their medical uses may be. The word comes from the ancient Greek word for 'purple'.

Porphyrins are large, flat molecules whose unique structure enables them to interact with light in a way that gives them their colours. The chemical has ancient history, Milgrom told me. When free oxygen from photosynthetic bacteria began to accumulate in the atmosphere at the end of the Archean eon, between 4000 and 2500 million years ago, it allowed the development of more advanced life forms by providing a more efficient means of generating biochemical energy. Later, large, fast-moving vertebrates (including ourselves) need a transport system to move oxygen around their bodies. Enter haemoglobin, the oxygen transport protein whose red colour comes from the iron-containing porphyrin haem.

Milgrom wrote for the *New Scientist* in the 1970s and '80s. He attended a talk David Dolphin gave on the theory that vampires might suffer from porphyria, and the *New Scientist* splashed it in its Halloween issue. In 1985, Dolphin presented his case to a reporter-packed meeting of the American Association for the Advancement of Science. This is an august organization. That it should discuss vampires was remarkable.

Dolphin highlighted one particularly severe form of the disease called congenital erythropoietic porphyria. It leads to disfigurement of the skin, causing the "nose and fingers to fall off" and the teeth to jut out in a menacing, animal-like manner. Sunlight made this worse and might have led sufferers to "venture forth only at night, as werewolves and vampires were said to do," Dolphin said. Skin may become highly photosensitivity and can blister. For some there is severe scarring and increased hair growth. Bacteria may infect the damaged skin. Sometimes it is like frostbite, and fingers may be lost. Red blood cells have a shortened life-span, and such patients often have anaemia.

The dramatic claim Dolphin made was that patients with porphyria might crave blood in an attempt to self-medicate their illness and "instinctively sought haem by biting human victims and a large amount of their blood." This claim was huge, as it assumed that someone who suffered from porphyria knew the cause of their disease – in 1985 you could not Google it – and so decide to take what might be a cure.

Dolphin also discussed what sufferers liked to eat and claimed that sufferers "might well have been afraid of garlic" since it "contains a chemical that exacerbates the symptoms of porphyrias." Milgrom thinks there is good evidence for this.

In the Royal Society of Arts café, Milgrom showed me two pictures of men who looked like lepers, in fact. The first was a Transylvanian called Matthias Petry who was the assistant of a famous chemist. His face was discoloured and his teeth prominent. He looked better than Dr Meyer Benz, who injected himself with 200 milligrams of hematoporphyrin and went out in the daylight. Meyer Benz's face swelled up and looked distorted and grim, a little like the Elephant Man.

There are remedies – obviously blood transfusions, and perhaps removing the spleen, which may reduce porphyrin production by the bone marrow.

Critics point out that Dolphin's claims were never published in the peer-reviewed scientific literature. In a 1990 article, Mary Winkler and Karl Anderson argued in *Perspectives in Biology and Medicine* that porphyria is not associated with blood craving, is not made worse by garlic, is not associated with haem deficiency and cannot actually be treated by ingesting blood. The authors were funded by the American Porphyria Foundation, who were annoyed that "sensationalism and superstition rather than science" have been responsible for porphyria's association with vampires. Lionel Milgrom's book, which covers his and Dolphin's ideas, however, has been published by Oxford University Press, which is not given to publishing either psychobabble or chemobabble.

The hypothesis that people who fear they have porphyria drink blood has one obvious flaw. How do they know that blood is what they need?

Milgrom explained to me that Dolphin's work and his own has led to some interesting developments in cancer therapy. When porphyrins absorb light, they can pass the energy on to oxygen molecules, thereby creating a highly reactive form of oxygen called singlet oxygen. This is highly damaging to tissue. If you can beam this accurately into a tumour, it can destroy it. So 'vampire biochemistry', as Milgrom calls it, offers a chance of real medical progress in cancer treatment.

During one of his mad episodes, George III threatened to kill his eldest son, the insufferable laudanum-quaffing Prince of Wales, who annoyed Jane Austen by interrupting her all the time and Byron for much the same reason. George III was neither a sadist nor a serial killer, but psychiatrists have been surprisingly slow to study the nature of any link between sadism, vampirism and serial killing.

In 1984, Herschel Prins, a social worker, surveyed forensic psychiatrists or psychiatrists interested in serious deviancy. He found, predictably enough, that vampirism was associated with "schizophreniform disorders, hysteria, severe psychopathic disorder, and mental retardation." He proposed four categories of vampirism, including 'complete vampirism' where individuals drank blood, necrophilic activity and necro-sadism. In other words, some vampires gorged on recently dead bodies. A decade later, Philip Jaffe and Frank DiCataldo added cannibalism to the list. It was not just fictional characters like Hannibal Lecter, who liked to reminisce about a nice slice of brain with a nice bottle of Chianti. Usually cannibalism happens in extreme conditions, for example when sailors are drifting after a shipwreck and there is no other food. But not always: the philosopher Bertrand Russell wrote some wonderful stories about cannibalism in *Satan in the Suburbs*. Psychopaths commit the very few cases of what one might call cannibalism in the suburbs – and psychopaths have many vampiric traits.

As I discovered when I made a film for Channel 5 called *What Makes Jeffrey Tick*, one much-used test for psychopathy uses 16 questions to decide where someone rates on the psychopath scale. The fifth edition of the Diagnostic and Statistical Manual of Mental Disorders (DSM-5) lists psychopathy as an antisocial personality disorder (ASPD). Psychopaths can be charming like vampires. They cannot form emotional attachments or feel real empathy with others. Vampires are more able to do this. Psychopaths are very manipulative and can easily gain people's trust. So does Dracula till he reveals his real intentions, and indeed Hannibal the Cannibal.

In real life, many notorious serial killers, including the late Ted Bundy and John Wayne Gacy and Dennis Rader (who said "Bind, Torture, Kill"), are unremorseful psychopaths. They see their victims as not really human but objects to be toyed with, tormented and killed. The link to Gilles de Rais is clear.

Very few real cases of vampire syndrome have been described, and the published reports that do exist refer to more conventional psychiatric diagnoses such as schizophrenia or as a variety of paraphilia. In his thorough history of Britain's asylum for criminal lunatics, Broadmoor, Gordon (who was medical director of the hospital) found no true vampires had ever been within its walls, though they housed many killers who dismembered their victims, and some even ate body parts.

Prins had discussed necrophiliac activity, and recent history has one notorious instance. In 1983, Nilsen, the so-called Muswell Hill Murderer, admitted to killing 15 men and boys and probably tried to kill seven others. Muswell Hill is a wealthy area of London, which was rather titillated by the story. Most of Nilsen's victims were homeless or homosexual men, whom he would typically meet in bars, He lured them back to his flat, usually offering drink or the chance of a bed for the night.

One of the psychiatrists who examined him while Nilsen was on remand discussed the case in confidence with me and showed me a draft of his report. It is not breaking that confidence to say my friend who had worked at Broadmoor was both shocked and baffled by Nilsen.

When Nilsen got his victims into his flat, he fed them and gave them food and alcohol. He then strangled them and then drowned them victim in his bathtub or his sink. He then dismembered the corpses, whose parts he sometimes put in a bucket of water, and often removed their internal organs. Nilsen masturbated as he viewed the nude bodies of several of his victims and engaged in sexual acts with six of his victims' bodies.

Fiction can be kinder than fact. In *Dracula*, the unfortunate Renfield, in an insane asylum and under telepathic control, serves the infamous Count. While not a vampire himself, Renfield consumes insects and rats in the belief that their blood will cure him. The psychiatrist Richard Noll coined the term 'Renfield's syndrome' in his book, *Vampires, Werewolves, and Demons: Twentieth Century Reports in the Psychiatric Literature* (1992b). Noll wrote a controversial book, *The Jung Cult*, which suggested Jung supported the Nazis and that he tended to think of himself as a saint. In my own *The Escape of Sigmund Freud*, I found evidence that he had, at the very least, done nothing to help Jewish psychoanalysts when the Nazis took power. This controversy is important, but not to this book.

Noll suggested that Renfield's syndrome is characterized by a 'blood-drinking compulsion' that "almost always has a strong sexual component associated with it," with blood taking on "an almost mystical significance as a sexualized symbol of life or power." He claimed that those with Renfield's syndrome typically start drinking their own blood, which he called auto-vampirism, when they were young. Then they progressed to drinking the blood of animals, or zoophagia, and finally on to full blood-drinking vampirism. Some old case histories suggested it started in childhood with an event that made a blood injury or the ingestion of blood exciting. After puberty, it's all about sex, straight, gay or bizarre. Drinking blood can also stimulate a sense of power and control.

In *Dracula*, Renfield ultimately betrays the Count and is killed by him rather than being turned into a vampire. In their paper, "Renfield's Syndrome: A Psychiatric Illness Drawn from Bram Stoker's *Dracula*," Régis Olry and Duane Haines argue that:

> Contemporary popularization of the types of behaviour exemplified by Renfield, such as programs/movies portraying vampires or werewolves, may actually serve a positive scientific purpose. While they do not get to the root of the clinical condition, and rarely or never offer a 'treatment', the observer is treated to a vivid impression (and hopefully some degree of understanding)

of the personal and societal torment that individuals with actual clinical conditions of similar types actually experience.

Characters suffering from Renfield's syndrome have made it on the screen. There is a splendidly bitter performance in Coppola's *Dracula*. On August 15, 2012, Renfield's syndrome was the subject of a video segment on The Huffington Post. There has also been a scholarly article in the *Journal of the History of the Neurosciences*.

In 2010 Megan White and Hatim Omar suggested:

> Emerging as an offshoot of the Gothic movement of the 1980s, today's contemporary Vampire subculture comprises individuals who claim to be "real vampires." Such individuals may engage in vampire-like behavior, including only emerging at night, sleeping in coffins, wearing fangs, and even blood-sharing. . . . The image of the vampire has changed throughout history from the monstrous, living-dead vampire in Bram Stoker's *Dracula*, to the alluring, romantic and compassionate vampire seen in Anne Rice's *Interview with the Vampire* and in Stephanie Meyer's *Twilight* series. As such, more individuals are drawn to vampirism, thus perpetuating the emergence of vampire cults.

In a Kentucky adolescent medicine clinic, White and Omar saw a 15-year-old white teenage male who had no past medical or psychiatric history. He had been cutting himself at school. He stated that he is "addicted to blood." He added that he always "liked the taste of blood." For the past 1–2 years he had cut himself to drink his own blood. He objected that "everyone is making such a big deal out of this, but it is not a big deal. It's not like I want to kill myself." He denied any emotional relief from cutting, denied changes in mood, sleep, appetite or energy level and denied he was suicidal or had homicidal fantasies. He used drugs liberally, including Adderall, Xanax, Klonopin and marijuana. He denied any association with a vampire group and stated that his friends and his girlfriend knew about his behaviour but thought it was 'weird' and did not participate in similar behaviour. He was neatly dressed in a graphic T-shirt, dark fitted jeans and studded belt and wore his hair partially covering his face. He remained very guarded and never returned after the first interview.

Two other patients with similar 'blood cravings' have been seen by physicians at the same adolescent medicine clinic, but all patients deny any involvement in vampire groups or cults. Still, White and Omar suggested that auto-vampirism might be "an emerging behaviour and possible acceptable coping strategy amongst the modern adolescent community."

There continue to be attempts at explanation. In 1998 in *Neurology*, Gomez-Alonso suggested that symptoms of rabies – such as a tendency to bite and an aversion to strong smells and mirrors – bear an uncanny resemblance to historical descriptions of vampires. He noted that the early vampire reports in the 1730s came a few years after a major rabies epidemic was recorded in Hungary.

Juan Gómez-Alonso, a neurologist at the Hospital Xeral in Vigo, Spain, says the idea struck him as he watched his first vampire movie on television nearly 20 years ago. He was intrigued when the movie's presenter quoted philosopher Jean Jacques Rousseau saying that vampires were real historical figures. "I watched the film more as a doctor trying to solve a difficult clinical case than as a spectator," he wrote.

There were reasons to diagnose vampires as rabid, Gomez Alonso added. They sleep badly and often have increased sex drives. Rabies is much more common in men than in women, as is supposed vampirism. The animals associated with vampires – wolves and dogs – were common rabies carriers at the time. In addition, bloody saliva sometimes drips from the mouths of rabies victims, as they have trouble swallowing.

The article produced a sceptical response, however, from Charles Rupprecht, chief of the U.S. Centers for Disease Control and Prevention. He noted that even if a rabid 'vampire' were to bite 100 people, only 5% to 10% might develop rabies. Gomez Alonso had got an irrational bee in his head, he suggested.

Given the fact that teenagers love vampires, one might expect to find a link between vampiric behaviour and self-harm. Those who blog about self-harm very occasionally say they have licked their wound to drink the blood, but few approve of the practice. One appalled self-harmer warned:

> don't, sounds real gross. Despite cutting myself for 7 years, I never did have a thing for the blood. Yes, it is bad. You could get iron poisoning if you drank enough of it. If your saliva is touching the wound, it's breaking down enzymes that helps repair the wound so that'll result in more blood/more time to wait until the bleeding stops.

One issue with linking vampirism to porphyria, mental illness or rabies is the calmness associated with vampires. The psychiatric literature research and the literature on cults both stress the violence of vampires and killers. With vampires the violence does not seem to be demented. Browning, for example, cited no cases where vampires lost control, which some serial killers do. Then, too, vampires nearly always drank blood from people who allowed them to do it.

Polidori's end was violent, but it did not involve anyone else, let alone the drinking of blood.

12

A MODERN OEDIPUS, BLOODLETTING AND THREE DEATHS

In the summer of 1819, Polidori fell from his gig. It destroyed him physically and psychologically. His behaviour became increasingly strange. His relationship with his father remained strained.

The accident contributed to Polidori's rapid decline. Harriet Martineau wrote that if he had 'happily' died when she knew him in Norwich, "he would have remained a hero in our imaginations. The few following years (which were very possibly all the wilder for that concussion of the brain) disabused everybody of all expectation of good from him." After his accident he produced very little. His long poem *The Fall of the Angels* was his only completed work after 1819.

Polidori's family were unable to help him recover. When a friend invited him to dinner on August 23, 1821, Polidori seemed more distressed than usual. He looked haggard and ate virtually nothing; he spoke in jumbled sentences and "appeared deranged in his mind." He said his friend would see more of the future than he would. When Polidori left his fellow diners, he shook one of them "so violently that it forced him to kneel." Restless as ever, Polidori came back a while later and then left again.

When he got home to 37 Great Pulteney Street in Soho, Polidori told his landlady not to wake him even if he were not up by noon. He also asked for a tumbler of water. The next day the landlady went into his room after noon. Polidori was deathly ill. She ran to get help, but by the time his friends came, Polidori was dying. They sent for two doctors, but when they got to his bedside, he was dead. His parents were heartbroken.

The coroner convened an inquest two days later. It returned a verdict of death by natural causes, but the verdict was controversial from the first. Many said the coroner – and the jury – were trying to spare the family. One of the jurors had been at school with Polidori.

Polidori's death was the first in a series of tragedies that affected everyone who had been at the Villa Diodati. The Shelleys left Britain in 1818 for Italy. Two of their children died before Mary Shelley gave birth to her only surviving child. In 1822, Shelley, who had still not had the sense to learn how to swim, drowned when his sailing boat sank during a storm.

In 1823, Byron decided to help Greece escape from Ottoman dominion. He had sold some land and settled his debts and then spent £4,000 of the proceeds refitting a fleet for the Greek rebels. There, Byron was not just interested in military plans. Continuing his homosexual career, he pursued his Greek page, but Lukas did not allow the poet to fall on him like a thunderbolt, as chambermaids and indeed so many young men had done years earlier.

Byron had the bold idea of attacking the Ottoman fortress of Lepanto, the site of a famous naval battle in 1570. Though he had no military experience, Byron assumed command of part of the rebel army. Before the fleet could sail and the poet could show he was a second Napoleon, however, he fell ill. His new physician, Julius van Millingen, resorted to the usual remedy of bloodletting, but that only made Byron weaker. Six weeks later, in April 1824, the poet caught a violent cold. Van Millingen decided on more bloodletting. Even in 1824, doctors knew it was vital to sterilize the instruments used in an operation, but van Millingen did not have the sense to do that. Byron got an infection and died of a violent fever on April 19. Poor Polidori at least had not killed his patient.

Byron's remains were sent to England, with his faithful manservant. The plan was to bury the great poet in Westminster Abbey, but the Abbey was not having that, given Byron's reputation of 'questionable morality'. It would take 145 years for the Abbey to relent. In 1969, a memorial to him was finally placed in Poet's Corner.

After Shelley drowned, Mary returned to England and devoted herself to bringing up her son and writing. She published historical novels, *Valperga* (1823) and *Perkin Warbeck* (1830), and the apocalyptic novel *The Last Man* (1826). After she wrote her last novel, *Falkner* (1837), she fell ill. She died in 1851.

The most miserable of them all, Claire Claremont, outlived them all. She died in 1879 after living unhappily in almost every country in Europe.

Gaetano lived for 32 years after his son died.

Polidori had been close to his sister Frances. Five years after he died, she married an Italian exile, Gabriele Rossetti. Their two sons, Dante Gabriel Rossetti and William Michael, were among the co-founders of the Pre-Raphaelite Brotherhood. As we have seen, William also edited the diary of his uncle, John Polidori. Frances' youngest child, Christina Georgina, became one of the most famous poets of Queen Victoria's reign.

The last chapter looks at Polidori's cultural legacy and the irony that a writer who was often so desperately broke created a character who has made millions for others. Buffy the Vampire Slayer could be called Buffy the Money Maker.

13

POLIDORI'S CULTURAL LEGACY

We have seen that Polidori complained the English were 'automatons'. Today psychology is heavily influenced by computer models of the mind and the possibility of conscious robots. We worry they may develop consciousness and wills of their own. Polidori's vampire can be seen as an early symptom of a deep-seated modern fear that we, too, might be soulless automata.

Vampires have become an industry. The great *New Yorker* film critic, Pauline Kael, categorized the essence of movies as 'bang, bang' or 'kiss, kiss'. She left out 'suck, suck'. *Twilight* grossed over $300 million; *Interview with a Vampire* $105 million.

Vampire movies are almost as old as the movies. The first notable one was *Nosferatu* (1922), starring Max Schreck as the evil Count Orlok. Schreck was an apt name for the actor, as it means 'fear' in German. The producers did not bother to buy the rights of Bram Stoker's *Dracula*, however, and his estate sued and sucked the producers dry, as it were. A court ordered all copies to be destroyed. In 1994, European scholars restored the film from five prints that had somehow survived. The next classic film was another adaptation of Stoker's *Dracula*. This time the producers paid for permission.

In 1936, when Universal released a sequel to *Dracula's Daughter*, the Nazis were in power in Germany. They were fascinated by the occult, named a military operation after werewolves (Project Werewolf recruited 5,000 young Nazis to perform secret operations behind enemy lines) and saw vampires as part of their folklore. They also used the old blood libel to justify their persecution of Jews. The libel, as we have seen, bore some relation to vampirism, especially for those who wanted to make the link.

The Nazis had to demonize the Jews, who were often successful professionals, and to promote notions of racial superiority, for which they found evidence in legends. They used, Nagl had claimed in an analysis, "a tremendous turning back of culture, away from the age of reason and consciousness, toward the age of a 'sleepwalking certainty', the age of supra-rational magic."

Hitler had a dowser – dowsing is an old technique where a special stick is waved, usually to find water – scour the Reich Chancellery for cancerous 'death rays' when he first took power. Before he flew to Scotland in the deluded hope of making peace with Churchill, Hitler's deputy, Rudolf Hess, consulted his personal astrologer. Himmler backed research on the Holy Grail and mediaeval devil worship and sent an SS expedition to Tibet in 1938 to investigate the ancient Indo-German 'Aryan' origins of Buddhism. Himmler also founded the SS Witches Division, who, alas, did not use broomsticks.

Eight years of work led the American historian, Eric Kurlander, to understand the extent of Nazi interest in the weird and the supernatural. In an interview, he said:

> There's evidence that many Germans and certainly some leading Nazis believed in supernatural beings and forces, especially in the distant past. Not that everyone in the party really believed in vampires and werewolves, I'm not going so far as to say that, only that there's a reason that they chose these tropes and the British and Americans, at least at that time, did not. Can you imagine Roosevelt or Churchill calling a major military operation Project Werewolf?

Maybe, but Kurlander forgot how the RAF used the name Vampire.

After the Italian dictator and Hitler's ally Mussolini was arrested, the Nazis released 40 experienced astrologers, tarot card readers, magicians and dowsers from concentration camps and brought them to a villa in Berlin's Wannsee, where the plans for the final solution were drafted. The leader of the occult experts was a magician called Wilhelm Wulf, or William the Wolf. Their task was to find 'Musso', as Clement Attlee, Churchill's deputy, called the bombastic Italian dictator.

Kurlander traces Nazi obsession with the supernatural belief to mystical theories which flourished in fin-de-siècle Austria and Germany. Weirdest of the weird, the Nazis were besotted by the World Ice Theory. In his 1912 book *Glacial Cosmogony*, Hanns Hörbiger argued with no evidence at all that white 'Aryan' man was not descended from the apes but rather came from 'divine sperma' brought to earth by meteors. These super sperm developed into the godlike Supermen of the ancient civilization of Atlantis-Thule, which employed parapsychology and mystical electricity. Some producer will surely spot the Hollywood potential of my next project, *The Apes and The Super Sperm*.

Hitler and other senior Nazis believed these peculiar beliefs, as did Carl Jung, to some extent at least. Julius Streicher, the editor of *Der Stürmer*, a paper that even Hitler had his doubts about, was convinced that he could 'smell out a Jew' at several metres. Hermann Goering's cousin Matthias was actually a competent psychoanalyst, but he refused to treat Jews because they were too 'other'. Goering, being an egomaniac, said he would decide who was a Jew.

Kurlander believes that Nazi reliance on magic encouraged the development of pointless 'wonder weapons' such as the V1 and V2 rockets, which killed many civilians but did not affect the Allied war effort. In 1943, he estimates 3,000 tarot-card readers were still working in Berlin alone. The British parachuted faked copies of the astrological magazine *Zenit* into Germany which contained pessimistic horoscopes for Hitler and his henchmen.

Goodrick-Clarke's book *The Modern Mythology of Nazi Occultism* describes Hitler and the Nazis as being controlled by a "hidden power . . . characterized either as a discarnate entity (e.g., 'black forces', 'invisible hierarchies', 'unknown superiors') or as a magical elite in a remote age or distant location." What made Hitler believe such fantasies is hard to pin down. He was an avid reader, and his library contained 6,000 books – no one has produced a reliable catalogue, but some were likely to be mythological and could have encouraged these occult fantasies.

Thirty years after World War II, Anne Rice added a crucial development and one which reflected the influence of psychoanalysis. She allowed vampires to look in the mirror. Louis is the first to describe his experience of seeing his vampire image. He is amazed, and it suggests to him that perhaps he does have a soul. He is appalled when he sees himself sucking blood from a rat.

Never having seen their reflections, it's no surprise vampires are desperate to see what they look like. When small children see themselves either in mirrors or on video they are often fascinated and laugh helplessly. Mirrors matter.

Anne Rice made the vampire more sympathetic and more modern. Interview with the Vampire became a successful film. Neil Jordan, who 'helmed' the movie, as Variety likes to put it, attracted an A list cast – Brad Pitt, Tom Cruise, Antonio Banderas and Kirsten Dunst.

There's still life in the genre today. The movie site IMDb lists 20 of the best recent ones. Many have used great stars and famous directors. There's even a small homage to Lugosi in Tom Hanks and Meg Ryan's comedy You've Got Mail, when a Dracula-look-a-like appears and Hanks teases Ryan about whether he is the date she is waiting for.

Ignoring the laws of physics, movie vampires can travel through time to bite Greeks, Romans, mediaeval monks, Victorian virgins and Wall Street wizards. Each neck is equal, but some necks are more equal than others. Virginal blood gives a special buzz. Cronos centres on a mysterious device which was designed to give its owner eternal life and which resurfaces four hundred years on. The result – the centuries are splattered with blood.

From Dusk till Dawn (1996) also managed to get some of Hollywood's finest. Two criminals take hostages, and then blow it because they take refuge in a place pulsing with vampires. The desperadoes forgot to check the premises. Chaos, blood, gore follow as Harvey Keitel, George Clooney, Juliette Lewis and Quentin Tarantino star.

Vampires also are sometimes the only ones left after the bomb had gone off or the aliens have taken over. Surviving, of course, brings them little joy. Where are they to get their next blood cocktail? I Am Legend (2007) also attracted a major star, Will Smith. The plot was apocalypse-plus. A plague wipes out most of humanity and turns the rest into monsters; the last hero in New York struggles to find an antidote.

There are 95 vampire films in preparation, including Wolf Man and one I can't wait to see, Turn, where Lyana, a compassionate vegan, is turned into a vampire and has to face the horrible reality that to survive she has to kill and suck blood.

Two television series, Buffy the Vampire Slayer and True Blood, as well as the movie series Twilight, have become iconic, and the prestigious egghead periodical, The Atlantic ran a headline, "Buffy Summers: Third-Wave Feminist Icon."

In 2009, Latoya Peterson, who edits Racialicious.com, a site that explores the intersection of race and pop culture, argued vampire tales "are not like the glossy look-but-don't-touch sexuality you see in 'Vogue'. They reflect our culture's deep ambivalence about women's sexuality and our obsession with glorifying chastity and sexual violence." The Twilight series makes sexuality dangerous and taboo. Peterson writes; "Sex equals bloodlust, and in general the rule is 'Just Say No!' – unless you put a ring on it." Bella Swan, whose name implies grace and purity, and Edward Cullen's first kiss ends when Edward smashes into Bella's bedroom wall to stop himself from doing more than pecking her on the lips. Bella and Edward only consummate their relationship three novels later after they marry, like nice normal teens.

Of Twilight, Peterson said "I don't think that it was Stephanie Meyer's intention as an author to force virginity down the throats of her readers." She then realized Meyer was an observant Mormon and asked if her characters had to "face punishment every time they act on a sexual feeling?"

By comparison, sex flows throughout *True Blood*. In season 3 of the HBO TV series, the very straight bartender Sam even has an erotic dream about vampire Bill Compton. Sookie, the blonde innocent, starts off a virgin, waiting for the right man. But once she has sex, she is a case of once bitten, twice not-at-all shy. Sookie soaks it up and loves to experiment. Unlike many heroines in horror movies, Sookie doesn't end up dead for her sexuality. She even enjoys allowing her vampire lover to bite her to orgasm.

Peterson argues that

> the vampire trend has created a space for a more in-depth discussion of sexuality than existed before. Most TV shows and movies don't come close to representing the complexity of real sexual interactions, but Edward, Bella, Bill and Sookie might be helping us get a step closer.

Last but not least is Buffy, the postfeminist superhero. Wisecracking, vampire-killing tough chick, Buffy Summers ran for seven seasons and developed a cult following. Buffy is independent, smart and incredibly physically strong, but still a schoolgirl. Later in the series, she's more mature but still wrestling with who she is and what she wants from life. Buffy has clever dialogue, the mid-battle banter and the witty one-liners fans love. There is, however, some controversy about whether Buffy is flawless as a feminist icon. Beight has argued – and I love the name of the learned journal in which her paper appears: *Sprinkle* – that the show opened a door but then did not push through it. In any event no new Buffy shows have been made for a decade and no other program has replaced it.

Buffy was created by Joss Whedon. Women's rights group Equality Now gave him an award for his courageous support of women's rights in 2006. He said that a woman kicking ass is extraordinarily sexy. He said piously that as a feminist, he had been compelled on a very base level by that archetype to create Buffy, who was no helpless virgin on a slab.

A final recent film has infiltrated the vampire into American history, making Abraham Lincoln a vampire hunter. The story is so weird it needs detail. In 1818, Lincoln's mother is murdered. Nine years later in 1827, a vengeful Lincoln tries to kill her murderer, but Barts, who is actually a vampire, overpowers him. However, before Barts can kill him, Lincoln is rescued by Henry Sturges, who explains that vampires exist, and offers to teach Lincoln to be a vampire hunter. Lincoln accepts. Sturges tells Lincoln that the vampires in America descend from Adam, a vampire who owns a plantation in New Orleans. Sturges also tells Lincoln of the vampires' weakness for silver and gives him a silver pocket watch.

After a number of narrow escapes, Lincoln discovers plans to turn the United States into a nation of the undead and that the slave trade keeps vampires under control, as vampires use slaves for food; if Lincoln interferes, the vampires will retaliate.

After Lincoln becomes resident in 1860, he and Mary have a son, William, who is later bitten by Adam's sister, Vadoma, who is also a vampire. The boy dies.

The Confederate President Jefferson Davis convinces Adam, the leader of the vampires, to deploy his vampires in what should be the final battle. Lincoln orders the confiscation of all the silverware in the area and has it melted down to produce silver weapons. Adam learns that Lincoln will transport the silver by train.

On the train, Adam and Vadoma attack Lincoln. During the fight, Adam learns that there is no silver on the train, but rocks. Lincoln kills Adam and escapes the train before it explodes. Meanwhile, Mary and some ex-slaves have transported the silver to Gettysburg.

The now leaderless Confederate vampires stage a final assault. Armed with their silver weapons, the Union soldiers destroy the vampires. During that battle, Mary confronts Vadoma, the vampire that killed her son, and kills her. Lincoln is offered the chance to become a vampire himself so that he can become immortal and continue to fight vampires, but Lincoln declines. I'm inclined to wonder how many recent Presidents accepted the offer and are actually vampires.

I look forward to the sequels – *Henry VIII, Vampire Hunter* and, since they wrote a book called *Why War?* together, *Einstein and Freud – Vampire Hunters*. Einstein shoots them with his relativity ray gun. And the rom-com where Buffy and Lincoln fall in love.

Recently Dracula has even been turned into a ballet, whose final act shows the undead initiating their newest victim. The struggle between the good and the undead climaxes in a sexually charged finale that leaves little to the imagination, according to the Charleston paper that reviewed the show. One imagines that some of the audience came en-fanged, having ordered them from Amazon, where Escapade Fancy Dress offers small deluxe fangs for sale.

The blurb is carat gold. Scarecrow Vampire Fangs are

> the most realistic comfortable fangs available! Easy, fast and every-thing included to customize the highest quality fang caps to your teeth. The permanent snap-fit mould created allows you to reuse for life without the need for any adhesive and no partial plate.

Dentists need a mention for those for whom fake fangs are not enough.

The most permanent method recommended for achieving 'fangs' is shortening one's front teeth while filing the canine teeth. Being responsible professionals, few dentists will do this, as it would weaken the structure of the teeth that are filed down. The second way is to have fang-like crowns placed over the canine teeth. Again, this is a more permanent option that won't be easy to remove and will change a canine tooth permanently. Most dentists will still refuse to do this, as it makes teeth vulnerable and more likely to chip or decay.

But there is a safer method – getting veneers that replicate fangs. They are completely aesthetic and do not damage the basic structure of the tooth.

I hope by now that I have explained the psychology of vampires and how they have changed in fiction and fact from demonic mon-sters to human beings who have many frailties, including a need for blood. Milgrom's work on porphyria is truly interesting, and we may find that the interest in vampires helps find new techniques for attacking cancer. The subject is, as this book has been, wide ranging.

Finally, we should return to Polidori. He has featured in *Highlander*, the *X-Files* and *Horrible Histories*. The title of one novel that features him,

Bite MeYour Grace, illustrates the point made at the beginning; the vampire is a gentleman who happens to have an unfortunate compulsion – or even fetish. In another novel, Lord Byron himself becomes a vampire and is hunted by Polidori who is armed with the usual stake. Usually poor Polidori is less heroic – for no good reason – and sometimes he has even been turned into a vampire himself, as in Hide Me Among the Graves.

Polidori has also been a minor character in a number of Franken-stein films. The unfortunate doctor usually gets murdered by the man monster. Polidori has been traduced in most of these works. He had many faults, but he was still very young. Who knows what he might have done if he had not been so depressed that he committed suicide?

FURTHER READING

Carpe Jugulum (Latin for "seize the throat", cf. *Carpe diem*). It is a comic fantasy novel by English writer Terry Pratchett, the twenty-third in the *Discworld* series. The book makes fun of the cliches of vampire literature and includes a reversal of the usual "can't be seen in the sun" vampire as the characters include young vampires who wear bright clothes and stay up till noon. Fun.

Two good non-fiction introductions are:

Dundes, A. Ed. (1998) *The Vampire: A Casebook*. Madison: University of Wisconsin Press.

Sherman, A. (2014) *Vampires: The Myths, Legends, and Lore*. Avon, MA: Adams Media.

REFERENCES

WORKS BY JOHN POLIDORI

(1815) An Essay Upon the Source of Positive Pleasure. In *The Vampyre and Other Writings*. Ed. Franklin Charles Bishop. Manchester: Carcanet Press, 2005, 39–45.

(1815) Oneirodynia (Somnambulism): Trans. with notes by David Petrain. *European Romantic Review* 21.6 (2010): 775–88.

Letter to Gaetano Polidori: 20 September, 1816. In *The Vampyre and Other Writings*.

(1819) *The Vampyre and Ernestus Berchtold: Or, the Modern Oedipus: Collected Fiction of John William Polidori*.

(1911) *The Diary of Dr. John William Polidori, Relating to Byron, Shelley, Etc.* Ed. and Elu. William Michael Rossetti. Elkin Mathews. And also (1975) *The Diary of Dr. John William Polidori*. Folcroft Library Editions This Diary Gives the Fullest Account of the Travel to Geneva.

Cajetan. Unpublished Play.

Polidori, A. (1847) *Osteologia, poema didascalico: copiato dall autografo manoscritto da Gaetano* (Polidori). Privately Printed.

WORKS BY LORD BYRON

A Fragment (1819) in *Mazeppa*. London: John Murray.

Don Juan (2004) London: Penguin.

Giaour (2009) in The Major Works. Oxford: Oxford University Press.

Thyraza (2009) in The Major Works. Oxford: Oxford University Press.

BIBLIOGRAPHY: WORKS BY OTHER AUTHORS

Atlanta Vampire Alliance (2007) The Vampire and Energy Work Research Survey: An Introspective Examination of the Real Vampire Community. Atlanta, GA: Atlanta Vampire Alliance [AVA].

Auerbach, N. (1995) Our Vampires, Ourselves. Chicago: University of Chicago Press.

Auerbach, N. (1998) Ellen Terry: Player in Her Time. Philadelphia: University of Pennsylvania Press.

Austen, J. (1817) Northanger Abbey. London: John Murray.

Bannister, D. Ed. (1975) Issues and Approaches in the Psychological Therapies. London: Wiley.

Barber, P. (1988) Vampires, Burial, and Death. New Haven, CT: Yale University Press.

Beight D (2014) Feminist Remix of Buffy the Vampire Slayer. Sprinkle, vol 7, 34–45.

Belanger, M. (2004) The Psychic Vampire Codex. Boston: Weiser.

———— (2007) Vampires in Their Own Words. Woodbury: Llewellyn Enfield.

Belford, B. (1996) Bram Stoker: A Biography of the Author of Dracula. New York: Knopf.

Bell, M. (2011) Food for the Dead. Hanover: Wesleyan University Press.

Benedetti, J. (2003) The Real Bluebeard. Stroud, UK: History Press.

Bennett, A. (1995) The Madness of King George. London: Faber and Faber.

Bettelheim, B. (1991) The Uses of Enchantment. London: Penguin.

Boucicault, D. (1858) The Legend of Devil's Dyke. Unpublished Play.

Braid, J. (1850) Observations on Trance. London: Churchill.

Brandreth, G. (2008) Oscar Wilde and the Candlelight Murders. London: Hodder Paperbacks.

Brown, C. (1831) Edgar Huntley. London: Henry Colburn, originally published 1799.

Browning, J. (2015) The Real Vampires of New Orleans and Buffalo: A Research Note towards Comparative Ethnography. Palgrave Communications 1, Article number: 15006.

Butz, M. P. (1993) The Vampire as a metaphor for working with child abuse XX American Journal of Ortho Psychiatry, l 63: 426–31.

Calmet, A. (2007) Apparitions. Ware, Hertfordshire: Wordsworth, first published 1746.

Carpenter, W. (1874) Principles of Mental Physiology. London: H. S. King.

Carter, A. (2016) House Training the Id. In Marina Warner, *Once Upon a Time*. Oxford: Oxford University Press.

Census of Hallucinations (1894) Publisher Unknown.

Clark, C. M. (1944) Clinical Assessment of Adolescents Involved in Satanism. *Adolescence* 29: 461–8.

Cohen, D. (2012) *Home Alone*. London: Robson Books.

——— (2018 in press) *The Development of Play*. Abingdon, UK: Routledge.

Coleridge, S. T. (1816) *Christabel: Kubla Khan, a Vision, the Pains of Sleep*. London: John Murray.

Conan Doyle, A. (1922) *The Case for Spirit Photography*. London: Hutchinson.

——— (1928) *The Coming of the Fairies*. Psychic Press.

Cullen, W. (1795) *Synopsis of Medical Nosology*. Philadelphia: Parry Hall.

Cutter, J. A. (2006) Vampire Cult Killings, 10 Years Later. *Orlando Sentinel*, 17 December.

Dante, A. (1977) *The Inferno*. Trans. Dorothy Sayers. New York: Penguin Classics.

Darwin, C. (1860) *On the Origins of the Species*. London: John Murray.

——— (1971) *A Biographical Sketch of an Infant*. London: Heinemann, originally published 1877.

Darwin, E. (1803) *Zoonomia: Or, the Laws of Organic Life*. Boston: Thomas and Andrews.

De Sade (1880) *Les prosperites du vice*. Bonneau.

Dolphin, D. (1979) *The Porphyrins*. New York: Academic Press.

Dowden, E. (1886) *Shelley*. London: Kegan Paul.

Engels, F. (1844) *The Condition of the Working Class in England Available* 2018. Create Space.

Esdaile, J. (1852) *The Introduction of Mesmerism, as an Anaesthetic and Curative Agent*. Perth: Dewar and Son.

Fortune, D. (2011) *Psychic Self Defense*. Aziloth Books, first published 1930.

Freud, S. (1929) The Future of an Illusion. In *Standard Edition of the Complete Psychological Works of Sigmund Freud*, vol. 20. London: Vintage Classics.

——— (1953) Three Essays on the Theory of Sexuality. In *Standard Edition of the Complete Psychological Works of Sigmund Freud*, vol. 7, originally published 1905. London: Hogarth Press.

——— (1955) The Uncanny. In *Standard Edition of the Complete Psychological Works of Sigmund Freud*, vol. 17. Trans. and Ed. James Strachey. London: Hogarth.

Ganz, T. (2009) Iron in Innate Immunity: Starve the Invaders. *Current Opinion in Immunology* 21: 63–7.

George, S. (2017) How Long Have We Believed in Vampires. *The Conversation*, 27 October.

Grady, F. (1996) Vampire Culture. In *Monster Theory: Reading Culture*. Ed. Jeffrey Jerome Cohen. Minneapolis: University of Minnesota Press, 225–41.

Gregory, L. (2009) *The Monk*. Vintage Books, originally published 1819.

Gomez Alonso, J. (1998) Rabies a Possible Explanation for the Vampire Legend. *Neurology* 51.3: 856–9.

Goodrick Clarke, N. (2012) *The Modern Mythology of Nazi Occultism*. London: Tauris Parke.

Gordon, H. (2012) *Broadmoor*. London: Psychology News Press.

Greenberg, S. (2008) Leibniz on King: Freedom and the Project of the 'Theodicy'. *Studia Leibnitiana*: 205–22.

Groom, N. (2010) *English Romantic Writers and the West Country*. New York: Palgrave.

Hamilton, W. (1853) *Discussions on Philosophy and Literature*. London: Edinburgh.

Halevy, A., Levi, Y., Shnaker, A., and Orda, R. (1989) Auto-Vampirism-an Unusual Cause of Anaemia. *Journal of the Royal Society of Medicine* 82: 630–1.

Hardy, A. (1973) *The Challenge of Chance*. London: Hutchinson.

Hardy, T. (1930, 1970) *The Collected Poems of Thomas Hardy 1840–1928*. New York: Macmillan.

——— (1994) *Collected Poems*. Ware, UK: Wordsworth.

Hayter, A. (1968) *Opium and the Romantic Imagination*. London: Faber and Faber.

Hergenjahn, B. and Olson, M. (2007) *An Introduction to Theories of Personality*. London: Prentice Hall.

Hitler, A. (1939) *Mein Kampf*. London: Hurst and Blackett.

Hobhouse, J. C. (1909) *Recollections of a Long Life*. London: John Murray.

Horbiger, H. (1993) *Glacial Cosmogony*. London: Belhaven, originally published 1912.

Huguenin, T. (1995) *Le 55ieme*. Paris: Fixot.

Irwin, S. (1982) *To Love a Vampire*. London: Carousel.

Jaffe, P. and Dicataldo, F. (1994) Clinical Vampirism: Blending Myth and Reality. *Bull Am Acad Psychiatry and Law* 22: 533–44.

Jentsch, E. (1906) Zur Psychologie des Unheimlichen. *Psychiatrisch-Neurologische Wochenschrift* 8.22 (25 August 1906): 195–8 and 8.23 (1 September 1906): 203–5.

Jones, E. (1931) *On the Nightmare*. London: L and V Woolf.

Jung, C. (1991) *The Archetypes and the Collective Unconscious*. Abingdon, UK: Routledge.

Kraft, E. R. (1897) *Psychopathis Sexualis*, vol. 30.

Kraus, R. F. (2008) Cliques and Cults as a Contributor to Violence in the School Environment. In *School Violence and Primary Prevention*. Ed. T. W. Miller. New York: Spiller, 215–25.

Kraus, R. F., Lane, T., and Heister, T. (1999) An Adolescent Vampire Cult in Rural America: Clinical Issues and Case Study. *Child Psychiatry and Human Development* 29: 209–19.

Kurlander, E. (2017) *Hitler's Monsters*. New Haven, CT: Yale University Press.

La Mettrie, J. (1912) *Man a Machine*. Chicago: Open Court, originally published 1747.

LaVey, A. (1992) *The Satanic Bible*. New York: Avon.

Laycock, J. (2009) *Vampires Today*. Santa Barbara, CA: Praeger.

——— (2010) Real Vampires as an Identity Group: Analyzing the Causes and Effects of an Introspective Survey by the Vampire Community. *Nova Religion* 14: 4–23.

Le Fanu, S. (2005) *Carmilla*. Paris: Zulma, originally published 1872 check.

Leibniz, G. W. von (1981) *New Essays on Human Understanding*. Trans. and Ed. P. Remnant and J. Bennett. Cambridge: Cambridge University Press.

Macdonald, D. L. (1991) *Poor Polidori: A Critical Biography of the Author of the Vampyre*. Toronto: University of Toronto Press.

Macdonald, D. L. and Scherf, K. (1994) Introduction to the Vampyre and Ernestus Berchtold: Or, the Modern Oedipus. In *Collected Fiction of John William Polidori*. Ed. D. L. Macdonald and K. Scherf. Toronto: University of Toronto Press, 1–29.

Malzieu, M. (2018) *Diary of a Vampire in Pyjamas*. London: Quercus.

Marx, K. (2013) *Das Kapital*. Paris: Wordsworth, originally published 1867.

Mellor, A. (1988) *Mary Shelley: Her Life, Her Fiction, Her Monsters*. New York: Methuen.

Mesmer, A. (1776) *On the Influence of the Planets*, unpublished doctoral dissertation.

Meyer, S. (2006) *Twilight*. New York: Little, Brown.

Milgrom, L. personal communication.

Miller, T. (2008) *School Violence and Primary Prevention*. London: Springer.

Miller, T. W. and Silman, M. (1994) Adult Non-Survivors: The Failure to Cope of Victims of Child Abuse. *Child Psychiatry and Human Development* 24: 231–43, 15.

Moore, T. (1835) *The Life of Lord Byron*. London: John Murray.

Murray, P. (2004) *From the Shadow of Dracula: A Life of Bram Stoker*. London: Jonathan Cape, 48.

Nagl, M. (1974) SF, Occult Sciences and Nazi Myth. *Science Fiction Studies* 1: 3.

Nodier, C., Carmouche, P., and de Jouffroy, A. (1990) Le Vampire: mélodrame en trois actes. In *Oeuvres dramatiques I: Le Vampire et Le Délateur, by Nodier*. Ed. Ginette Picat-Guinoiseau. Paris: Librairie Droz, 35–41.

Noll, R. (1992a) *The Jung Cult*. Princeton, NJ: Princeton University Press.

——— (1992b). *Vampires, Werewolves and Demons: Twentieth Century Reports in the Psychiatric Literature*. New York: Brunner and Mazel.

Oppawasky, J. (2011) *Sexual Abuse*. Bloomington, IN: Xlibris.

Orwell, G. (2014) *Such, Such Were the Joys*. London: Penguin.

Peterson, L. (2010) On Buffy the Vampire Slayer. Racialilicios.com.

Planché, J. R. (1986) The Vampire: Or, the Bride of the Isles. In *Plays by James Robinson Planché*. Ed. Donald Roy. New York: Cambridge University Press, 45–68.

Preyer, W. (1895) *The Mind of the Child*. New York: Appleton.

Prins, H. (1994) Vampirism-Legendary or Clinical Phenomenon? *Medicine, Science, and the Law* 24: 283–93.

Rhine, J. B. (1950) *New Frontiers of the Mind*. New York: Penguin.

Rice, A. (1997) *Interview with the Vampire*. New York: Ballantine.

Rieger, J. (1963) Dr. Polidori and the Genesis of Frankenstein. *Studies in English Literature, 1500–1900* 3: 461–72.

Rossetti, W. M. (1975) Introduction. In *The Diary of Dr. John William Polidori*. Folcroft Library Editions, 1–24.

Russell, B. (1961) *Satan in the Suburbs*. New York: Penguin.

Rymer, J. (2015) *Varney the Vampire*. New York: Dover.

Schaffer, T. A. (1994) Wilde Desire (1994'). *ELH* 61: 381–428.

Schneider, A. (2015) *Soul Vampires*. Pennsauken, NJ: Bookbaby.

Shaw, G. B. S. (1966) *St Joan*. Harlow, UK: Longmans.

Shelley, M. (1996) *Frankenstein*. Ed. J. Paul Hunter. New York: W.W. Norton.

Southgate, B. C. (1992) The Power of Imagination. *History of Science* 30: 281–94.

Stern, M. (2011) Anne Rice on Sparkly Vampires, 'Twilight', 'True Blood', and Werewolves. *The Daily Beast*, www.thedailybeast.com/anne-rice-on-sparkly-vampires-twilight-true-blood-and-werewolves

Stiles, A. (2006) Cerebral Automatism, the Brain, and the Soul in Bram Stoker's *Dracula*. *Journal of the History of the Neurosciences* 15.2: 131–52.

Stoker, B. (1897) *Dracula*. Archibald Constable and Company.

——— (1906) *Personal Reminiscences of Henry Irving*. London: William Heinemann.

——— (1997) *Dracula*. Ed. Nina Auerbach and David Skal. New York: W.W. Norton, originally published 1896.

Storey, M. (1997) *Robert Southey*. Oxford: Oxford University Press.

Sully, J. (2018) *Studies of Childhood*. London: Forgotten Books, originally published 1892.

St Yves, M. and Bellerin, B. (2010) Vampire or Pinocchio scénario délictuel chez les délinquants sexuels. *Revue Internationale de criminologie et de police technique et scientifique* 52.2: 179–89.

Tittmus, R. (1970) *The Gift Relationship*. New York: New Press.

Tolkien, J. R. R. (2013) *On Fairy Tales*. New York: Harper Collins.

Twitchell, J. (1987) *The Living Dead*. Durham, NC: Duke University Press.

Udovitch, Mim (2000) 'Buffy the Vampire Slayer': What Makes Buffy Slay?, *Rolling Stone*, May 11.

Van der Bergh, L. L. and Kelley, J. (1964) Vampirism. *Archives of General Psychiatry* 11: 543–7.

Vasbinder, S. (1984) *Scientific Attitudes in Mary Shelley's Frankenstein*. Ann Arbor: UMI Research Press.

Viets, H. R. (1961) John William Polidori, M.D., and Lord Byron: A Brief Interlude in 1816. *New England Journal of Medicine* 264: 554.

Warner, M. (2016) *Once Upon a Time*. Oxford: Oxford University Press.

White, M. and Omar, H. (2010) Vampirism, Vampire Cults and the Teenager of Today. *International Journal of Adolescent* 22: 189–95.

Williams, D. J. (2008) Contemporary Vampires and (Blood-Red) Leisure: Should We Be Afraid of the Dark? *Leisure/Loisir* 32: 513–39.

——— (2009) Deviant Leisure: Rethinking 'the Good, the Bad, and the Ugly'. *Leisure Sciences* 31: 207–13.

——— (2013) Social Work, BDSM, and Vampires: Toward Understanding and Empowering People with Nontraditional Identities. *Canadian Social Work* 15: 10–24.

Williams, D. J. and Prior, E. (2015) Do We Always Practice What We Preach? Real Vampires' Fears of Coming Out of the Coffin to Social Workers and Helping Professionals. *Critical Social Work* 16: 1–21.

Wilson, K. (1985) The History of the Word 'Vampire'. *Journal of the History of Ideas* 46.4: 577–83.

Winkler, M. and Anderson, K. E. (1990) *Vampires*, Porphyria, and the Media: Medicalization of a Myth. *Perspectives in Biology and Medicine* 33.4: 598.

Young, R. (1990) *Mind, Brain, and Adaptation in the Nineteenth Century: Cerebral Localization and Its Biological Context from Gall to Ferrier*. New York: Oxford University Press.

Zabow, T. (1983) Clinical Vampirism: A Presentation of 3 Cases and Re-Evaluation of Haigh, the Acidbath Murderer. *The South African Medical Journal* 63: 278–81, 3.

Printed in the United States
by Baker & Taylor Publisher Services